Footloose

Or How to Run Away to Sea

Tim Bull

ISBN: 9798864937105

Imprint: Independently published

Cover design by: Tim Bull

Main Image: Shutterstock / Amanita Silvicora

Praise for author

The most honest, hilarious and compelling book about buying and living on a boat I've ever read. How to stop dreaming about running away to sea and do it! — **Judy, Sailing** *Fair Isle* **(YouTube)**

***

Are you looking to lose yourself in a book again? This is the one... A great story and very entertaining to read. — **Henk-Jan,** *MV Lady Liselot* **(YouTube)**

***

To be honest, the book was unexpectedly good. — **Jasper, Author's Son**

For Karina, together we can do anything! For Ella and Jasper, we love watching your adventures unfold. For my fellow cruisers, you make living on a boat worthwhile.

RIP Rosie 2012-2023, Best boat dog ever

Disclaimer

This book is a memoir, but it's also meant to entertain. No one wants to read a verbatim account of what the author ate for breakfast on Friday, 9th of July 2021 (most likely cereal). It reflects the author's present recollections of experiences over time. Some names and characteristics have been changed, some events have been compressed, and some dialogue has been recreated, usually with less swearing. The author may appear wittier and more competent than was the case at the time. Importantly, while there is boating advice offered in this memoir, the author is not an instructor, and you follow any advice contained within at your own risk.

Contents

One

The end

"We can't change the wind, but we can set the sails differently." — Aristotle

As Karina and I rode our tender[1] *Tilly* back to our boat *Matilda*, we watched a sailboat swinging violently around its chain.

"Are they anchored?" I asked her. "That boat's moving weird. Can you see the chain at the bow? Maybe they are trying to lift the anchor?"

A woman came forward to the bow of the boat and looked down at the chain, worry creasing her forehead. She threw her arms into the air and then returned to the helm.

The boat swung around on the anchor chain again, jerking suddenly as she motored forward, then in reverse. It stopped, and she walked quickly back to the bow, peering down at the water.

"Could be that she's just checking the anchor's set?" I mused.

"She looks like she's stuck. Why don't you go and ask if she wants some help?" said Karina. "Drop me back at the boat, then you go over and see if everything's okay."

After three seasons at sea together and 28 years of marriage, she knows me far too well. I wouldn't be able to relax until I figured out what was going on.

I dropped Karina back to *Matilda* along with our dog Rosie and then headed over to the sailboat.

The woman at the bow watched me warily as I approached.

---

1. A mini boat for your big boat.

"Hey, how's it going?" I asked.

"Ahh, I think my anchor's stuck," she responded. "Are you New Zealanders?"

"No, Australians."

"Oh, I wasn't sure; I couldn't quite make out the flag. I lived in Australia for a few years."

"Cool. I'm Tim. Nice to meet you. Can I help at all, or are you fine?"

"I'm Jasna," she replied, relaxing and beaming a grateful smile as she realised I wasn't going to be an arsehole and yell at her for anchoring nearby. "Some help would be very useful. I'm solo[2] and can't see how the chain moves when I'm on the helm to get it unstuck. I was thinking maybe I'd have to dive on it in the morning, but if you could hop up the front and point out the chain for me, we might be able to work it free."

As I pulled alongside her boat, Jasna grabbed the painter[3] and tied off *Tilly* to a stanchion[4], and I used the shrouds[5] to pull myself onboard.

"Shall I take my shoes off?" I asked.

It's always good etiquette to establish that early on when boarding someone's boat.

"No, don't worry, she's filthy anyway. You go up front and tell me which way to move, and I'll steer the boat."

I leaned over the bow and saw the chain disappearing underneath the boat. Using large arm movements, I indicated the angle at which the chain was lying, and Jasna manoeuvred the boat slowly backwards. As the chain went slack, I started to winch it in.

crunch

Suddenly, the boat stopped, and the chain pulled taut. Yup. It was stuck under something alright.

"Try coming forward slowly now," I yelled back towards the helm. "Ok, forwards again... backwards... hold there...."

Each time the boat moved, I winched in a little more slack, gradually lifting the chain off the bottom and hopefully away from whatever it was getting caught on.

---

2. Sailing on her own without crew.

3. A rope used to tie up a tender so you don't lose it!

4. Essentially a fence post on the deck of a boat that holds the lifelines — lines that run around the boat to prevent you falling overboard.

5. Strong stainless steel wire that stops the mast falling down.

"Ok, forwards again..."

There was another metallic scraping sound, and the chain jumped forward and then hung loose.

I quickly brought in the sudden slack. "I think we've got it! Yes, I can see the anchor now."

Jasna came back up to the bow to check the progress. "That's a relief. I'm so glad I didn't have to dive on it. Hang on... the chain is starting to catch on the windlass[6]."

The windlass wasn't feeding it properly back into the anchor locker as the chain came up. I mentally kicked myself; I really should have checked that.

She quickly fed the loose chain into the anchor locker as I brought the anchor the rest of the way in.

"I could have waited until morning and freed it with diving gear, but I hate it when you're stuck like that; you just never know if it will hold properly overnight," she said.

With the anchor safely stowed, our thoughts moved to getting her boat secured away for the night.

"Strictly speaking, I think you're not supposed to anchor here. Would you like a hand to tie off to one of those mooring buoys over there?" I pointed at the mooring field nearby, where *Matilda* was safely secured.

It was off-season, but our brief experience with the Croatian authorities was that they are sticklers for the rules. Solo like she was, it was understandable why she chose to anchor. Tying off to a mooring when you're alone is difficult, especially on these buoys with a heavy chain link as a pendant.

"That would be great; I appreciate it."

Five minutes later, once her boat was safely tied to a mooring buoy, I invited her to join Karina and me aboard *Matilda* for a drink after she finished settling in. There was no need to ask twice.

"I'll see you in a few minutes," came her enthusiastic reply.

Onboard *Matilda*, a drink in hand, we all chatted together about the things we'd seen and what brought us to this moment here on a boat.

Within a few moments of meeting her, it was clear Jasna was experienced. She charters her boat and runs a small sailing school, but as we later found out, she has also written

---

6. The big silver winch at the bow of a boat which contains gears to haul up the chain.

several successful books on sailing. They cover her time in the South Pacific, where she also appeared in a British TV documentary about living aboard a boat.

Her anchor sticking is no reflection on her skills but more a reality we've come to learn and appreciate. If it can go wrong on a boat, at some point, it will. She had a plan B and C to get safely free. My timely offer of help just meant she didn't need to use them.

"I love this community," she said, "everyone is so willing to help each other out. It made things a lot easier for me that you knew what you were doing."

It's a nice feeling being recognised by someone like Jasna for a degree of competence.

But boy, have we come a long way from the beginning. Karina, who previously knew nothing about boats, could now recognise a vessel needing assistance. For me, a formerly desk-bound keyboard jockey, it was becoming someone with skills to offer in a pinch. We've both grown to where we feel confident that we belong and can stand up and work alongside others with more experience in the cruising world than ourselves.

As I explained to Jasna, we're not the people we used to be.

***

It's never clear where the story really starts. But one beginning is when we were living in Silicon Valley. Just south of San Francisco, California, in the USA.

If there's a goal in tech circles beyond "change the world", it's all about the money. And not just any money. "Fuck you money." There are various definitions of what this might be, but it's generally accepted that it's enough to tell your boss to fuck off and not need to seriously worry about working again.

The challenge is that no one will tell you when that time is. There's absolutely no point in earning fuck you money if you never say fuck you.

The dirty little secret in Silicon Valley is that it's a roller coaster that everyone wants to ride again. I've met founders who've made hundreds of millions of dollars, and yet they all constantly strive to do more. Not necessarily earn more; the money at that point is just a way of keeping score. The sort of person who relocates to The Valley just for the money isn't going to last.

The people who succeed in The Valley thrive on challenge. Every switchback or loop on the roller coaster is merely another obstacle to overcome. It starts simply. A desire to "go work in The Valley". Soon, it's "work for a unicorn", "go join a startup", "found your own startup", "get some users", "get a round of funding", "get 1 million customers", and then "get major funding."

If you get thrown off along the way, you get right back in the queue to ride again, challenging yourself to go further and faster.

Even if you make it to the end, usually via a buyout or an IPO[7], there's always another ride. Once you're lucky, twice you're good[8]. Now, the goal is to prove that your previous success wasn't just luck, but it was you who brought something to the table. You personally made a difference.

For each measurable step of success, there's still one more to reach for. "You're investing in a sports team? That's cute; I'm launching cars into space."

Of course, almost no one makes it that far. The reality is that we each grind away at some vision, either because we genuinely believe in it or because the hint of the money is enough, only for the company to be acquired, absorbed and shut down by a competitor. And that's if you're lucky. The most likely outcomes are that you either end up a wage slave at a global behemoth with dubious morals or you grind away at a smaller startup, only to get kicked back to the start of the ride when the funding dries up.

Silicon Valley thrives on enticing the best of the best to ride again. Failure is worn like a badge of honour. Still, in reality, it's a sucker mark — shorthand for an individual willing to subject themselves to a high degree of employer and investor abuse. It's a game you can never win as there's always another goal to chase, another million to seek or another idea the world can't possibly survive without.

For a system that glorifies the mavericks, it doesn't particularly like people who want to think outside the box. It's a never-ending carnival game looking for the next rube to come along and bet, with the fickle whim of consumers driving the hands that move the shells. Today's killer app is tomorrow's feature, ruthlessly stolen and tacked on to an existing mega company.

To keep you at the grindstone, artificial incentives are created. Employee vesting and share schemes are yet another lottery ticket. You've got to be in it to win it. If you leave now, you won't keep your shares (but let's not talk about dilution, investor preferences

---

7. Initial Public Offering - a listing on the stock exchange, where (unless you're pets.com in the 2000's) the investors make bank.

8. This is the title of a book by Sarah Lacey published in 2008. The desire to succeed and succeed again remains as true today as it was then.

and multiples, or the probability these shares will never actually be worth anything). The handcuffs look golden, but if you scratch the surface, you quickly realise they are poorly gilded tin.

But when a basic house in Silicon Valley costs over one million dollars, you don't have a choice. The only option is to keep chasing the carrot at the end of the stick, hoping you one day catch a bite.

Despite all this, it's a glorious game! It's crazy fun, it's energising, it's intoxicating and yes, even sometimes financially rewarding. Working in Silicon Valley was some of the best years of my working life, and I spent time with amazing people I'm proud to call friends, but eventually, it wore thin.

Behind the glamour and glitz, you start to feel the pointlessness of it all and realise that, just maybe, it's time for a change. There's a way to win, and it's to get out of the game.

At least one beginning of this story is when Karina and I decided to stop the roller coaster and step off the ride.

***

Still, even that doesn't explain why boats. For that, there's an even earlier beginning. This story starts with a dream.

I've been fascinated with boats from an early age, but I never even learned to sail until I was 45. Which probably isn't that strange, considering I've mostly lived in arid, desert climates far from the sea. Growing up in South Australia, there was a local beer ad with the line "From the driest state on the driest continent on earth". As a child, my experience of volumes of water was severely limited.

My sense of adventure, though, was limitless. A fervent imagination, a love of escape through reading, and living overseas in Jordan, in the Middle East during my pre-teen years left me with an outsized desire for adventure and to try something new.

But not just any adventure, the dream of boats was always there. One of the earliest books I remember is Little Tim and the Brave Sea Captain, by Edward Ardizzone. It's the tale of a young boy who stows away on a ship and works hard to earn his place. Even now, when I think back on it, I still recall images of Little Tim sitting out on deck, the camaraderie and working together to overcome adversity in a storm. That thought of "running away" and "making it on your own" came through.

A few years later, attending an English school in Jordan (another arid, dry, desert climate), Swallows and Amazons by Arthur Ransome was popular among my friends. It's a classic tale in the vein of the Famous Five, a quaintly English story of inter-war period children having adventures and solving mysteries, but with boats. We also liked to imagine that we were sailing free, navigating the world under our own power. Those of us who claimed some experience sailing at the tender age of 10 developed some serious street cred.

One friend, James, allegedly had an uncle who owned a boat, and he claimed to have spent his holidays sailing. He spoke confidently enough about the parts of the boat; that's called a mainsail[9], that's a jib[10]. Not to be outdone, I recalled the summer a year or two earlier when I'd spent all of about 15 minutes on my uncle's Hobie Cat[11]. I could be an expert, too. We both attempted to surpass each other, speaking knowledgeably about things we knew nothing of, and endlessly drew sailboats in class whenever there was an excuse to create art.

Even today, I still remember feeling like an imposter. Despite my bravado, I knew nothing about boats and even less about what they looked like. But that's never stopped a 10-year-old. As we tried to outdo each other, my drawings resembled large watermelon slices floating on the water with a stick in the middle and two triangles hanging off each side. I could lie now and tell you that we were savants who designed a sloop rig from scratch, but the boats we drew would have sailed poorly, if at all. Our jibs' bottom corner (clew) pointed into the wind, not away. I suspect now that James had about as much real practical experience on boats as me.

Two family holidays allowed me to spend time on the water on a self-driven house-boat on the Murray River. In Australia, these houseboats are large and unwieldy. Huge floating pontoons with an apartment on board, no boat license required. But I still recall the excitement of standing out on the front deck as we cruised up and down the river, exploring the billabongs[12] by canoe, and the feeling that this was different from the everyday. It was high adventure and further fuelled my dreams of a life at sea.

---

9. The big triangle sail on a sailboat.

10. The smaller triangle sail, towards the front of the sailboat.

11. A very popular small catamaran (twin hull) sailing boat.

12. A branch of the main river, forming a large pond.

In my teenage years, the dream turned to travelling through Europe. Rather than simply flying there, I wanted to make the trip without flying at all. Elaborate plans were made to hitchhike from Adelaide in South Australia to Darwin in the Northern Territory and, from there, try to catch a boat going to Singapore. The desire to emulate that childhood book and run away to sea was real. The dream of exploring by boat was still alive. To make your way via the unconventional and go where there are no roads, to live free and explore at a whim; it's an idea that gets deep into your blood. It never really goes away. But, for a time, as the increasing reality of work and relationships took over, my focus instead turned to other things.

They say the future is what happens while you're making plans. Karina and I met at a friend's 18th birthday party. She was the most interesting person in the room, someone I'd not met before from outside my friendship circle. A breath of fresh air, intelligence, and ambition in a room full of drifters[13] whose most pressing concerns were the next party.

She'd arrived with another guy, someone I knew from the occasional teenage hang-out together, but it was clear from the moment I spoke with her there was a significant mismatch. I later learnt she'd only come with him under pressure from her parents, who wanted to see her getting out of the house and doing "normal" teenage things. To keep the peace, she accepted his invitation to the party and walked into my life.

We spent the night chatting, and within a few weeks, we were dating. We've been inseparable ever since. While the initial desire to live on a boat is mine, in many ways, this story is ours. This dream would never have happened without Karina supporting me, grounding my increasingly wild ideas, and helping me make them a reality. And equally to put forward her vision and wishes for our life together, too.

In 1994, we were married, then relocated to Sydney, where I satisfied the urge to be on and under the sea by learning to scuba dive. Karina has never been one for adventure sports, preferring adventures without the sports component. But she took to cocktails on a boat, weekends away and snorkelling the Great Barrier Reef like a pro when she joined me on a few liveaboard scuba diving holidays in the Whitsundays. My urge to spend time at sea was satisfied, and perhaps a tiny seed was planted for her that the idea could be fun.

We travelled to Europe together. I never managed the complete avoidance of flying I'd originally planned, but it was still full of adventure. Together, we flew into China

---

13. Including me.

and caught the trans-Mongolian train from Beijing through Mongolia and across Russia. A brief stop in Hong Kong, visiting villages on small fishing islands by local ferry boat, rekindled the flame. How cool would it be to live on a boat, cruise, and travel to islands like this?

Reflecting on this time, I've realised just how special Karina is to our success as cruisers. Rereading our travel diaries today, it's clear how we both approached the same events with different perspectives. I always saw the next big adventure, seeking the challenge of travelling through former communist countries not long after the fall of the Berlin Wall. Karina kept us grounded and focused on the practical side of things.

While she sometimes wrote about feeling uncertain and stressed, placed way outside her comfort zone, she also spoke of how my confidence meant she believed nothing was outside our abilities. She always thought we could rise together to meet whatever life threw at us on the road. Together, we dreamed big. With my desire to push the envelope and Karina's ability to keep us grounded, we make a great team. These traits have proven to be essential to the success of our cruising life.

After the grand train journey ended in St. Petersburg, Russia, we headed to Greece and travelled by ferry to several islands. There was Paros, Anti-Paros, Naxos and Santorini. This was 1997, and the fleet of self-chartered boats that now infest the islands wasn't as prominent, but the sea is still an ancient constant in Greece and the hub of island life.

Memories of walking through small fishing ports and dreaming of living on an island surrounded by crystal blue waters would stay with us both for years to come. We've always talked about island life together.

Back to Australia, and our lives continued. Two kids and an expanding career with frequent work travel to not-quite-so-exotic locations like Tampa, Florida, satisfied my urge for adventure for a time, but it never entirely faded away. Then, my energy was diverted into founding a tech startup and Karina's in holding down a sense of normalcy for the family while I flirted with bankruptcy. Eventually, via a last-minute acquisition that saved us, we made our way to Silicon Valley as a family, where the story really begins.

Two

The Seed

"To live is the rarest thing in the world. Most people exist, that is all."
— Oscar Wilde

I vividly remember the moment when the dream turned into something concrete. It was New Year's Day in 2016, and I was sitting in bed in our house in Belmont, California, where we'd lived for four years.

Once again, I was daydreaming about running away on a boat.

Truth be told, years of hard work and hard eating were taking their toll. I was significantly overweight and, in retrospect, far unhappier and more stressed than I wanted to let on to the family and myself. With the endless grind of that startup roller-coaster wearing me down, the thought of abandoning our lives in the USA to sail the seven seas was becoming all-consuming.

But every time we talked about it, it came back to the same problem – while Karina was also keen for a change, she didn't share that particular dream and regardless, the kids needed to complete high school. I felt trapped by circumstance and responsibility—something needed to change.

Lying in bed, thinking about what my New Year's resolutions should be, it suddenly hit me. "Maybe if I want to run away with Karina and live on a boat, I should learn to sail first?"

You'd be forgiven for thinking this would be the first thing you'd do after a lifelong desire to explore the world by sea. But as I've continued to learn, people are wired weird.

We self-sabotage all the time. It's far more comforting to have a big, unobtainable dream than to actively pursue it and fail.

Now, having made my own way into this lifestyle, it's something I see all the time in online groups about sailing. Everyone wants to role-play at being a potential liveaboard sailor. They ask endless questions, digging into the nitty-gritty of what boat, what's available, what systems should be on board and offering advice. Yet, they've failed to take the most basic of steps and learn to sail.

Up to that moment, I was no exception, a dreamer without doing.

Suddenly, a light switched on in my head. As small and insignificant a step as it seems now – here was something I could do to move towards the lifestyle I dreamed of.

I should really fucking learn to sail.

A quick Google showed several sailing schools in the San Francisco Bay Area where I could easily take the first steps, a more practical assessment to see if I even liked it or not. I spoke to Karina.

"Go for it," she said.

The sailing school in nearby Redwood City was highly rated and American Sail Association (ASA) certified. The ASA courses are a structured introduction to sailing, with modules that take you from your first steps on a boat to chartering your own and beyond. It's worth noting that the ASA is nothing unique. There's also US Sail in the USA, and the British RYA (Royal Yacht Association) offers a very well-regarded sailing education program throughout Europe, the UK, Australia and other parts of the world. Most countries have their specific licensing organisations and sailing schools, too. It doesn't matter which one you pick. Just pick one.

Fast-forward two months later and two days after my 45th birthday, I was on a boat on the San Francisco Bay, learning the basics of sailing for the first time. Finally, some 35 years after that schoolboy dreaming, I knew which way a jib should go.

I consumed all the theory books and annoyed my instructors with endless questions to the point that one pulled me aside and said, "You're good at the book learning stuff, but at the end of the day, you need to feel it."

Sailing and, indeed, boating is a mixture of science and art. I've come to appreciate this more, but at the time, I needed to be told to stop overthinking every small thing and to take the time to feel what the boat was telling me. The theory is important, but the magic is that it's you, a couple of ropes to set the sail and the fickleness of the winds and the tide that get you where you have to be.

That next year, I spent almost every weekend on the water. And every Wednesday, too, crewing on boats racing in "beer can[1] " races. I took additional courses, building my knowledge, and regularly chartered small 27-foot (ca. 7 metre) Catalinas up and down the South Bay with anyone I could talk into sailing with me.

This included Karina and the family. Which, in retrospect, was a mistake if my goal was to convince her to liveaboard with me.

If you're yet to go sailing, you may not be familiar with the degree to which sailboats can heel or lean as they head upwind. As the pressure of the wind builds on the sails, the boat can tip dramatically to one side.

Now, this is perfectly normal and, for most sailors, part of the fun. But for novice sailors, it can be a make-or-break experience. It's hard to envision cocktails on the deck and living at anchor while you're sailing in a small boat where nothing stays still. There's a reason one old sailing adage says, "Gentlemen don't sail to windward."

Karina's reaction was clear. I could enjoy going out in all weather on the bay if I wished, but she wouldn't be a part of it. For a time, it seemed that the dream of living aboard and cruising the world would go unfulfilled.

Thankfully, plenty of people were still willing to come sailing with me. Work colleagues, people I met through the increasing levels of sailing courses I was taking, or just other racers in the sailing club. There was never a shortage of someone wanting to get out on the San Francisco Bay.

My skills continued to grow. When I couldn't find friends to sail with, I would single-hand the small boats myself. I grew to love the challenge of being away cruising for four hours of an afternoon alone, free to experiment with the trim[2] and learn to feel the boat.

All too frequently, my confidence outgrew my actual abilities. Another novice sailor and I spent an embarrassing 5 hours with the boat stuck in the mud, waiting for the tide to lift us free after sailing too close to the edge of the channel. My son, who had finally agreed to try sailing with me again, was also aboard that day. He never let me forget it.

"I'd go sailing again, Dad, but I don't have 5 hours to spare."

---

1. So-called because back in the day, you used to be able to track the progress of the race from the trail of used beer cans.

2. Tightening and loosening the various ropes that control the sails. It impacts how efficient (aka fast) you are.

This misadventure did little to convince the rest of the family that coming back out on a boat with me was a good idea.

Despite these hiccups, I did continue to improve. The club had some 35-40 foot (ca. 10.5—12 metre) boats available for charter, and after a few trips with more experienced sailors, I successfully sat the club check-out exam so I could use them too.

Unsurprisingly, none of this did anything to slow my desire to liveaboard full time. I completed several weekend trips with friends, sailing from Redwood City up under the Bay Bridge, around Alcatraz and on to Sausalito. We would stay at a marina overnight, then sail back again the following day. The dream was still alive as I imagined doing this on my own boat.

And that might be where the story ends. Me, continuing to sail as a hobby, gradually gaining more experience and perhaps doing a few charters occasionally, all while unable to convince Karina that there was something to this lifestyle.

***

The breakthrough that changed our course was a family holiday to The Netherlands. We chose The Netherlands for many reasons, but at least in part because it is where Karina's father was born before he emigrated to Australia.

Initially, we were considering an RV[3] holiday, something we'd done before and enjoyed in the USA. But after much research and a bit of begging, I convinced the family we should try a canal boat holiday instead. We'd charter a self-drive barge to explore the canals, finally living aboard together for two weeks.

Not only did it feel like an authentic way to explore the countryside and villages of The Netherlands, but the sheltered waterways meant that there would be very little in the way of waves. Ultimately, what sold it was the fact that, on a flat-bottomed barge, there would be no heel at all.

The holiday was a great success. It combined the joy we'd felt on previous RV holidays with the novelty of a boat. What both experiences have in common is the cosy, comfortable feeling of everything at your fingertips. It's taking a holiday, with all the fun of new

---

3. Recreational Vehicle / Campervan. Basically any vehicle too big for the village you're trying to drive it through.

scenery and discovery, while at the same time, bringing many of the comforts of home with you.

The barge had a major unexpected benefit, too. RVs are big, unwieldy, and impractical to drive, excluded from the centre of cities and towns because of their size. In the US, the spiritual home of the "road trip", holidaying in an RV consists of moving a bus-sized monstrosity down massive freeways from trailer park to trailer park on the outskirts of the cities and towns.

Sure, occasionally, you get to go camping, but there's a reason that many full-time RV'ers in the USA drag a vehicle behind them; it's the only practical way to get to and explore most places easily.

With a barge, it's the opposite. The canals restrict where you can go, but you typically have a prime location in the centre of town when you get there. The canals are the historical lifeblood of the trading centres they were developed to serve.

We would stop the barge for the night in a historic town centre like Alkmaar and moor there for little money. Instead of being trapped thirty minutes or more away on the outskirts in an RV, we were in the heart of it all, staying on the canal with the comforts of home, right next to hotels charging hundreds of euros a night. Still, to this day, we look back on this holiday as one of the best we've done as a family.

Yes, there were moments of stress; boats, particularly barges, can be large, unwieldy, and slow. This is especially true when you've gone the wrong way down a canal and have to reverse several hundred metres back out again!

I also had a long way to go as a skipper. My instructions were frequently unclear and poorly understood during difficult moments like navigating a lock. As the moment's stress rose, I was prone to shouting, something I always hated happening to me when I was crewing on racing yachts. Unfortunately, it's a trend among inexperienced (and occasionally just plain bad) skippers. If what I said didn't make sense, repeat it, but this time louder!

A lesson I'm still learning to this day is the need to properly and clearly instruct the crew before an emergency arises. Equally, the crew (a.k.a. the family) weren't always on board with what it means to be crewing, either! Boats aren't democracies, but families aren't necessarily paid employees or passionate sailors.

Overall, though, despite the occasional hiccups, we all came to love that sense of discovery and the joy of moving from town to town.

Finally, I'd delivered an experience that matched what I felt and shared it with Karina in a form she wanted more of—drifting slowly down a canal, stopping at a local bakery, all while exploring the history of quaint old towns. This was a life we could live together. We had found a style of boat life we could agree on, a barge on a canal.

With the holiday complete, we made our plans. After five more years of work in the US, once the kids completed high school, we would sell up and move to Europe, and eventually, when we retired, a barge. In time, I'd get my boat life, and Karina would get her comforts of home, a boat that didn't heel and an ever-changing view. The promise of fresh French croissants and Dutch cheese didn't hurt either.

***

Plans are easy to make but oftentimes harder to execute.

I find joy in thinking about the things we could do and mapping out how to make it happen. Executing can be much more challenging — as the myriad of failed projects under my belt will testify. Perhaps if the world had stayed the same, we might still be in Silicon Valley, trapped on the treadmill by the lure of more money. We could be continuing to chase the next big break while waiting for our daughter and son to finish college. If they chose to remain in the US, we might decide not to leave.

But the world wasn't about to let anyone stand still.

As 2019 came to a close, our son only had six months of high school left before he'd be off on his own adventures — either to college or back to Australia to find work. Although we didn't intend to quit our jobs yet, the family home felt large, and we began to think about downsizing and moving into an apartment in a more urban centre.

Something we missed from our home in Australia was walkability. In Belmont, it was impossible to go anywhere without taking a vehicle. The idea of a smaller apartment in the nearby city of San Mateo with shops at our doorstep was appealing. It seemed like the change we needed while we adjusted to life without the kids and continued to plan the next stage of our lives.

We also felt, incorrectly, as it turns out, that the housing market couldn't possibly continue its upward trend. By November 2019, we were convinced that prices were approaching the peak, so we decided to prepare our house for sale and put it on the market in February 2020.

December 2019 saw the whole family on holiday in Jordan, returning to a place that was a big part of my childhood. We have many memories of that holiday, but one that sticks out is watching the BBC World Service on TV around New Year's Eve.

We thought little of it, sitting in that hotel next to the Dead Sea, listening to the first rumours of a concerning new virus that was emerging from Wuhan in China. The memory formed more from the delight of hearing English-speaking news after a couple of weeks on the road. The news item was more an idle curiosity, something to discuss on the car journey, and we had little idea that anything would come of it. Of course, none of us genuinely knew how life would rapidly change.

Fast-forward two months, and Covid-19 now had a name. Most people I knew were becoming increasingly concerned by the reports of lockdowns in Wuhan and greater China. With this happening in the background, Karina and I moved with our son into a rented apartment in San Mateo, and our house was staged and ready for sale.

Selling a house is always stressful, but as stock markets began to crash on the news Covid-19 was spreading outside of China, everything began to feel very uncertain. Italy went into lockdown, people started to panic buy, and we began to wonder if we should pull the house from the market. Perhaps we had called it right the year before; the housing market was going to tank — but maybe we'd missed the window to sell?

Instead of the positive buyer reception we had from our first buoyant open inspections, now, potential buyer after potential buyer was pulling out. On the day we took offers, the US stock market crashed, and we only received one serious bid. To our great relief, the offer matched our asking price after some negotiations, BUT the buyer added a condition. They had to sell their property first.

With little option, we decided to accept. Day by day, more and more countries went into lockdown, and the thought that the sale of our house might collapse altogether was an increasing concern. Suddenly, the NBA cancelled its competition. Covid-19 was continuing to dramatically impact our lives in increasingly unexpected ways.

Fortunately, right at the deadline, our buyer found a buyer for their property, and the sale went through. We turned out to be partially correct. The market did dip. The buyer of our house sold theirs at a discount to close their deal. Since then, the housing market rebounded strongly and has continued to grow. We didn't care; we were out and had our cash in the bank.

***

Karina and I worked for progressive tech companies, so it's no surprise that our employers acted quickly. Very early on, as Covid-19 spread throughout California, our companies immediately banned all travel, and we were told to start working from home.

It's surreal to remember those early days of the pandemic, but it was a strange period. We all knew very little about the disease, how it spread, or how to treat it. All we knew was it was dangerous, and it was spreading fast.

Shortly after our companies switched to working from home, San Mateo County issued its first broad lockdowns. Now, we were not just home voluntarily; we were in our tiny new apartment, locked down for real.

Working from home is something I've always been able to do at will. I don't mind it, but it's also not my preferred means of working either. I thrive off the contact and interaction with other people.

As a software development manager, most of my job was coordination and team management. It revolved around conversations and communications with various people internally on my team and with other managers. Working from home takes all the worst parts of that job and jams it into a video conference call, while the fun part of interacting and working with people face to face is removed.

As the weeks turned into months, the stress built up. The company decided Covid-19 required a reduction in force, a move that I disagreed with. Many heated conversations and arguments over video calls followed until one day, Karina came into my office (the table at the end of our bed) and simply said, "You know, you just don't sound like you're having fun anymore".

It was a moment of pause. Instead of waking up excited to head to work and ride that roller-coaster, I realised I was dreading the endless video calls and the lack of human interactions. At some point, the excitement of trying to solve the unsolvable had turned into the feeling I was beating my head against the impossible.

There was also a strong sense of déjà-vu from earlier startups. That nagging feeling that no matter how hard we try, no one wants what we're building, and we don't know what that is anyway.

When you're called out like that by someone close to you, you have to listen. I took a literal step back from my desk. We went for a walk in the local park and decided this was it. We had our plan; we had money in the bank from the house and enough scattered investments that we could step back from work for several years, potentially permanently.

Our "professional" working careers had reached a natural end; it was now time to say "fuck you", to stop existing and start living. We were ready to step off the roller-coaster, head to Europe and go live on a boat.

Three

Uprooting

"Twenty years from now, you will be more disappointed by the things you didn't do than those you did. So throw off the bowlines...sail away from safe harbor...catch the trade winds in your sails...explore...dream....discover." — Mark Twain

When the goal is to move on to a boat, you know you will need to downsize. And then downsize again. Surprisingly, it turns out that getting rid of things is addictive.

It starts as a slow and difficult process.

We attach ourselves to things and give meaning to "stuff" that holds no intrinsic value apart from the emotional value we layer onto it. They are hard to let go of.

We know in our hearts that dead Grandma's kitsch lobster-themed salad bowl is priceless, but the brutal disconnect is that in the harsh light of the neighbourhood boot sale, no one wants to pay 50 cents. It's tough out there.

Other things are easy. A pair of faux Mexican-themed flower pots, given to us by dear friends as a wedding gift, were finally disposed of. While our tastes and decor had long left them behind, physically, they travelled with us from house to house. Now, with no way they'd fit into the two-suitcase limit we'd allocated ourselves, we finally had the excuse to let them go.

No matter how sentimental, no one will begrudge you for disposing of a flowerpot when you're trading the life you know for travel and a boat. They may not understand why you want to live on a boat or be able to make the decision themselves, but they wish that they could. It's liberating.

Stuff accumulates fast, too! This wasn't the first time we'd reduced to almost zero possessions. Only nine years earlier, we'd left virtually everything behind when we moved from Australia to the USA. Strangely, that first time felt easier. Then we were letting go of furniture we'd purchased as students, cheap tables and chairs — the sort of furniture that would be from IKEA these days if it had existed in Australia back then.

Now, it hurt more.

Establishing a household in the US with money in the bank allowed us to carefully curate what we wanted to purchase. Vintage mid-century modern pieces that we were very proud of. Each was a treasured possession, scoured and hunted down online or from a few favourite stores. Letting them go was difficult, but the economics spoke for themselves. It wasn't worth shipping them back to our "permanent home" (my parents' cellar) in Australia. They had to go.

There is a light, however. With each tough decision made and every vintage chair sold, it gets easier and easier. Until one day, you're looking at a slightly used cardboard box, asking yourself, "Can I sell that?"

Suddenly, it becomes a game. How much money can I make? How much can I actually sell? What piece of crap I no longer need can make me a buck?

Sure, it's just an empty cardboard box, but package a few of them together, and you can offload them for $5 to Dave-down-the-road, who's moving house. Even if you can't sell it, there's always someone willing to come and take it off your hands without you even leaving the house.

A pile of random kitchen utensils becomes a "Value starter kitchen set for college students", and before you know it, half a dozen college Mums are vying to buy it.

You get ruthless in unexpected ways. Yeah, you can have the saucepan, but you have to take the paper towel holder with you, too. You don't want it? Sorry mate, but I've got someone willing to take both, and I'm not interested in separating them.

The money is fun, but frankly, by this point in the process, I'm just happy to have one less thing to dispose of.

I no longer care if the item I just ruthlessly bundled didn't make it past our wheelie bins at the end of the drive. At that point, it was your item you were throwing away and your guilt. I'd manage to find it a home. Plus, I didn't have to carry it out the door!

You lose yourself deep in the game. Now it's all about capturing an extra few cents, and soon, just how low do we have to go to move Grandma's kitsch lobster that no one should ever actually want or need[1].

I've spoken with plenty of people who've made this change and sold up to travel the world, and they all say the same thing. There's at least one thing you wish you'd kept and twenty you stored that you should have just sold.

Ultimately, we reduced down to two suitcases and two carryons. These four bags, the net result from offloading nine years of suburban life with teenagers, became all the possessions we would carry with us as we set off for Greece and our new boat life.

***

needle scratch

Back up a second here. Greece? It's not renowned for its canals[2].

When the decision was made to quit — to say "fuck you" and run away to sea — the initial plan was simple. Move to The Netherlands, buy a boat and liveaboard on the canals. The choice of The Netherlands was easy, undertaken without too much thought. We enjoyed the holiday we took there, so why not repeat that experience more permanently? We also assumed that Karina's Dutch passport and the fact we've been married for 25+ years would make it easy for us to get residency.

The Dutch government would like to disagree.

It quickly became clear that the process was more complicated than anticipated. For a Dutch citizen to sponsor a non-Dutch (i.e., me) partner for residency, they must establish that they can support the partner. This is usually done by checking your income on past tax returns. While technically, Karina is Dutch and has the passport to prove it, she's never lived or filed taxes there.

For Karina to sponsor me to live permanently in the Netherlands, we hit two major problems. The first was that she would have to establish herself. She'd have to find a job, earn some income, file a tax return, etc., all of which would take around 12 months to

---

1. I jest, the kitsch lobster salad bowl was shipped back to Australia. That thing is priceless.

2. Although it is renowned for one very famous one. The Corinth Canal. Given that's only a few kilometres long and surrounded by walls 50 metres high it would be a pretty boring place to live permanently on a boat.

complete, to prove she lived in The Netherlands so that she could sponsor me. The second issue is that while she was doing this, the advice was I would be unable to stay with her more than 90 out of every 180 days.

Let's just say that Karina was less than thrilled with the idea of quitting work, only to have to find a job in a foreign (to her) country. In a place where, despite her nationality, she doesn't speak the language. All while I spent twelve months swanning around the world, travelling and potentially even buying and living aboard a boat without her. The deal was always that we'd quit together.

Fortunately, we found a solution. While The Netherlands, or any European Union (EU) country, can impose restrictions on its citizens, EU law means they can't impose restrictions on EU citizens moving from other countries. EU law guarantees all their citizens free right of movement, including for their non-EU spouses.

As an Australian married to someone with a Dutch passport, I'm well qualified as a "non-EU-Spouse". Living together in the EU became straightforward. We could relocate anywhere we liked in most of Europe; we just couldn't easily move permanently to The Netherlands[3].

With that understood, we reevaluated our options. Northern Europe was ruled out as too cold, and the interior countries didn't have enough sea side, which led us to the Mediterranean. Once we started looking at Greece, it quickly became our preferred destination.

While it wasn't the canals of The Netherlands, it had many features of the life we sought. With between 1,200 – 6,000 islands (depending on what size you start counting), of which around 200 are inhabited, there are endless places to explore—small ports to stay in, placing you in the centre of the town and community. The travel distances are typically short, and in many locations, the seas are relatively calm and peaceful, and of course, there's spectacular swimming!

It was ultimately the swimming that sold it; the idea that we could stop somewhere and jump off into the water was compelling. We could have instead chosen the canals in France, but having been forced to consider things further, it turned out Greece was where we wanted to be.

---

3. We've since met other couples who have experienced the same challenge, for example a Danish person with an Australian spouse. It's easier of them to live anywhere but Denmark, however we could live there easily if we wanted!

While it was a change, it was one that Karina could support with one condition. No sailing boats. She, too, fondly remembered our time in Greece and was excited to explore it in more depth... or should that be breadth? The depths might be the wrong direction to explore on a boat...

Within a few weeks of the decision to quit, we were on our way to Greece. The detailed plan, well, that would come later. For now, it was as sophisticated as "get residency and buy a boat".

***

Arriving in Athens, the first thing to understand is that it's a city of two halves. There are the sanitised tourist districts, all Ancient Greece, street markets, hip bars, cafes, and tavernas. The sights that most tourists experience in their two days between arriving and departing for the islands. It's a fun, dynamic European city ready to titillate your senses with a gritty urban edge.

Then there's the real Athens that its people experience every day. It's raw, uncompromising and doesn't give a shit about your tourist sensibilities. In the city's centre, around the edge of the tourist zone, it's an assault on the senses. A concrete jungle coated in layers of paint and street art, crumbling buildings, apartment blocks and a gridlock of traffic.

It's a riot of vegetable markets and pedestrians. Trucks with loudspeakers blaring as they try to buy or sell goods. Clusters of mopeds block the footpaths outside cafes while their drivers wait for the next delivery order.

It's an acquired taste, something that challenges you to love it. Over time, you come to feel the rhythm of the city and appreciate its flawed grace, its raw life and uncompromising energy.

After 16 hours of travel time, it's confronting.

In August, the city is stiflingly hot. Even arriving at 2 am, the air felt too thick to breathe, and we were sweating in the car as we were delivered to our Airbnb by our host. The heat was still rising off the asphalt road and radiating from the concrete of the buildings.

"We're here", announced our host as he parked illegally next to a police riot bus.

The police were turned out in full riot gear, spilling out over the pavement. Several of them carrying assault rifles stood guard at the corners of the street block.

"It's okay," he says, sensing our consternation. "We're next door to the offices of a political party; it's very safe."

The level of visible riot gear and weapons on display suggested that this might, in fact, be a lie. Perhaps it's my Australian sensibilities, but the more weaponry on display, the less safe I feel.

The illegal parking hardly warranted a glance by the police, who were all staring at their mobile phones. Walking into the building, we took a closer look. Rather than alert, they seemed barely awake. Their riot shields a convenient wall to lean on as they wasted away the night. In Athens, nothing is ever quite what it seems. It was becoming clear that the rules weren't what we were used to.

The next morning brought further clarity. Stepping outside our apartment into the glaring sun, the police were still present, and the riot bus was still parked out front. But in the light of day, it was even clearer there was no sense of urgency.

Each small square of shade held a cluster of police, all sweating in their riot gear and balaclavas while madly sipping on their iced coffees, the ubiquitous Greek Freddo Cappuccino[4]. The act of guarding was simply being done because it was always being done rather than through any obvious actual necessity.

As we walked around the streets, it felt desolate. Shop after shop was closed, something we initially attributed to Covid-19, but we later learnt that during summer, two things are at play.

The first issue was that we'd arrived in the traditional holiday period of mid-August. Each year at this time, most shops shut down, and Athenians flee the heat, returning to their ancestral island homes and villages en masse.

The second is that in the summer heat, Athenians take the traditional "quiet hours" of 2–5 pm very seriously. What hasn't been closed due to holidays shuts down as people rest up during the hottest part of the day.

The area of the city we were in may not have been pretty, but it was not abandoned. It highlighted just how much we needed to learn about the rhythm and pace of our new home. Like every place in the world, Athens has its own culture and way things are done.

We had our feet on the ground, but there would be a lot more to learn as we moved to tackle step one of the master plan – sort out residency.

---

4. A cold, iced espresso coffee with milk.

***

The word "bureaucracy" originated in France, but its spiritual home is definitely in Greece. The image of a "bureau", the French word for office or desk, combined with the Greek word "kratos", meaning rule or political power, sums up the seemingly endless officials you need to navigate to get things done.

It's not strictly the fault of the person behind the desk. There are convoluted rules, processes and procedures that must be followed, and they didn't write them.

As non-Greeks, it's nearly impossible to understand. It all makes Arthur Dent's journey to the planning commission[5] in "Hitchhiker's Guide to the Galaxy" seem mundane.

Occasionally, the rules are so arbitrary they make no sense. At the heart of every Greek person's experience is KEP, the ubiquitous Citizen's Service Centre in every town and suburb that governs almost any interaction you might have with the government.

I've literally gone to KEP to pay a bill without an appointment, and a sympathetic attendant waved me through to the right queue. Having failed to bring some necessary paper, I was instructed to go collect it and return it immediately.

Less than thirty minutes later, I returned with the correct paper in hand, only for the same attendant that half an hour before had waved me through with good grace to scream, "Not possible, you must make an appointment."

"But you let me through here thirty minutes ago! I just need to see that man over there and give him this paper."

"No, this cannot happen – you must make an appointment."

I made the appointment.

While, in theory, it is possible to establish residency without a lawyer, the reality during Covid-19 was that you needed a fixer. Someone who knows the process and speaks the language to help you navigate the network of agencies you'll have to deal with to make it happen while the rules and procedures are changing every day. Ultimately, we required someone to help us save time with the proper guidance or, occasionally, the right smile.

---

5. When asked if he found the planning permit, Arthur replied... "Yes," said Arthur, "yes I did. It was on display in the bottom of a locked filing cabinet stuck in a disused lavatory with a sign on the door saying 'Beware of the Leopard.'" — Hitchhikers Guide to the Galaxy, Douglas Adams

As the lawyer we worked with said, "The worst thing about Covid-19 is all these masks; it means someone with a pretty face like Katerina can't always just smile and get things done. It all used to be so much easier."

While Greek women are frequently highly educated, it's also fair to say that women's rights in the workplace haven't advanced as much here as in other European countries yet. Misogyny is common.

In addition to the fixer, you also need to remove your sense of humour. The language barrier is too much, and the nature of the work too tedious to attract people who find humour in us describing ourselves as fun-employed[6].

Having established ourselves in a new country three times now, the process is always a Rubik's Cube of problems to solve. Labyrinthine bureaucracy is not just a Greek issue, but it was more frustrating this time with the language barrier and Covid-19 challenges.

The challenge goes something like this. You need Official Document A (say an electricity bill) to prove residence so you can open a bank account. To open an electricity account to get a statement with an address, you need to have Official Document B (say a lease), which, of course, you can't sign without Official Document C, a bank account. Which you can't open without Official Document A.

When you persist, you will always find a solution. It might be a little used document that the bank staff aren't familiar with (which they've never seen before because everyone has an electricity bill) or a willing landlord to write a short-term lease for cash without a bank account. However you crack the egg, eventually, you'll make the omelette. You have to take the time and be creative in finding the right way to approach it.

An additional complication is the many pointless seeming steps along the way. Greece still suffers from the aftereffects of the financial crisis and the deep austerity measures they had to follow. It impacts things in interesting ways. A classic example is how a second copy of documents is created when issuing an original official document. Rather than simply providing you the original and filing a copy, the newly created original document is returned to you.

You take the original document outside the office to one of the many little stores that have popped up to service this need and pay cash to make a photocopy. With the original and the copy in hand, you then queue again to return inside the building and hand the

---

6. Half the reason we now say we are retired is because officials recognise that people who aren't working are either unemployed, or retired. For some reason they object to 50 year old unemployed people entering their country.

copy back to the officer who first processed your application (and hope they haven't since gone on break).

Even in the Californian Department of Motor Vehicles, which until Greece was my benchmark for pointless bureaucracy, they at least have a photocopier. In Greece, paper and toner are expensive, but raw human resources and inefficiency are cheap. The cost of creating the copy is passed on to the consumer. Austerity is served by saving the price of a photocopied sheet of paper at the expense of an hour or more of the service consumer's time.

The wheels turned slowly, but they did turn, and eventually, we had our residency completed. With step one complete, "get residency", it was time to begin step two of the master plan. Buy a boat.

Four

Lost

"Anywhere, provided it be forward-- farther still farther into the night." — David Livingstone

W e had no idea what to expect when starting the boat-buying process. If pressed, I would have told you I expected it to be a bit like buying a car. We'd visit some fancy marinas with boats on display, each with a precise price sticker in the window. We'd kick... well, not the tires, but maybe the fenders[1]? Ask a few pertinent questions, check a few online reviews and then decide that yes, this is the car... I mean boat... for us.

Yeah, it's nothing like that. There's a million different ways it's not like that. I say now that buying a liveaboard boat is a little more like buying a house... If the home you want to buy has been covered in tarpaulins, and everything has been disconnected for 12 months, including the sewers, power, and water.

I should say that boat buying is an experience unto itself and one that you need to live to fully understand and leave it at that. Instead, I will try my best to help you appreciate it.

The first misconception is that instead of a beautiful marina, it's more likely that the boat you are interested in is on "the hard", a generic term meaning anywhere you store a boat on land.

---

1. Rubber "balloons" you hang from the side of your boat so you can hit things... or so that things that hit you bounce off.

One thing all on "the hard" locations have in common is that they are butt-ugly. No one stores boats on prime waterfront. It's always a crappy piece of industrial foreshore or a dusty compound outside of town. Wherever it is, "the hard" will be covered in junk, bits of old boats, empty oil containers and dusty boats in various states of maintenance and decay.

Not only has the boat you are there to see been physically removed from the water but it's also had random wooden planks jammed against the hull to prop it up and prevent it from toppling over.

If you're lucky, there's a scaffold to climb and enter it, but more likely, there's a rickety ladder, stolen from another boat, that you'll need to climb to get onboard. This ladder will be propped up on a piece of wood and requires a degree of gymnastic ability to not only climb it but also pass safely onto the stern of the boat.

If it was a house, it's most likely been staged to look its best. No one stages boats. Typically, the boat is filthy. This is partly because boat storage yards are harsh environments but mostly because cleaning boats is neither trivial nor cheap. Most sellers tend not to bother with cleaning in the early tire kicker stages.

The most likely reason the boat is filthy is that the owner left briefly at the end of the previous season, expecting to return shortly. But, because of Brexit and Covid-19, they have been unable to return and decided to sell instead.

Rather than being presented in a pristine state, the boat will still have the owners' underwear strewn on the bedroom floor, half-opened containers of food in the kitchen and condoms in the drawers. All things we've literally seen on boats for sale.

The next major problem is that while there are many boats for sale worldwide, once you start limiting by some key features, must-haves and price, there's a very limited supply.

When buying a house, you'll usually think about the area you want to be in and then look at the available homes in that location. Most likely, the houses will be clustered together, so you can easily tour all of them in an afternoon.

With boats, you focus on the models and features, which will produce a concise list. Because boats are pretty mobile, that short list could be spread across the Mediterranean or the globe.

Early in the search, you might assume that visiting the boat before entering negotiations is the right thing to do. This can become expensive quickly.

Despite Athens being the centre of the Greek world, most boats suitable for liveaboard use are stored at the extremities. Frequently, this is because it's both more attractive to travel in these areas and cheaper to keep the boat away from Athens. You'll quickly waste a lot of money travelling to remote island locations to visit a boat, only to find that the photos were outdated after arriving.

According to every seller we've met, everything on their boat is 100% maintained and in excellent condition. It's just that nothing is connected right now, so you can't test it, but don't worry, it's the BEST conditioned boat of its kind in the world.

"What do you mean, you want to see the maintenance receipts[2]? Don't worry about that; we have them; it's just that right now, we don't know where they are."

After visiting a few boats, you'll see the benefits of requesting some essential documentation and conducting some simple negotiations before you arrive, rather than just jumping on a ferry or plane.

Despite all these challenges, if you decide the boat seems reasonable, you'll want to proceed with properly testing everything. This means the boat must return to the water so you can conduct a sea trial.

You've already agreed the price, right? No? Okay, forget it – it's never going to happen.

Let's be clear here. Moving a boat from the hard back into the water is not cheap. There's probably some essential maintenance that needs to be done beforehand. Maybe the motors are in pieces as part of an overhaul and waiting on parts?

Before the seller goes to the expense and effort of prepping the boat, they will want to know that you are serious. You have to agree on a price upfront — BEFORE KNOWING IF ANYTHING WORKS — then pay 10% of that price as a deposit. Then, and only then, will the seller launch the boat so you can see that it all works properly. Hint – it probably doesn't.

Back to our house analogy. It's a bit like agreeing the price for a house, putting down a deposit and then paying for a building inspector and a plumber to come and inspect it. Just to make sure that the house is up to the standard promised. Remember that in this house analogy, you've only seen it with no gas, electricity or water and, of course, covered in 12 months of dust. With a boat, the equivalent to the building inspector and plumber is a licensed marine surveyor and an engine mechanic at a minimum.

When the boat is back in the water, you'll probably find that the seller wasn't completely honest and that this is NOT the best-conditioned boat on the market. There's

---

2. We've since discovered the lack of receipts could just mean that the work was done "off the books". Tax evasion is a national hobby in Greece.

every chance it will need a significant amount of money spent on it to get all the things that they assured you were working to work. You now have to decide. Do I buy it, or do I walk away? This decision MUST be made at the time of the survey.

As the survey uncovers issues, a good result, counter-intuitively, is an obvious, catastrophic failure. This makes the choice to walk a simple one.

Should you decide that the problems uncovered (and there WILL be problems uncovered) aren't too onerous, you need to inspect the boat out of the water to measure moisture and check the through-hulls[3] and propellors. As the potential purchaser, you are the one who must pay to have the boat removed from the water again so that all the systems you couldn't get at while it was in the water can be adequately inspected.

"But", you might say, "surely you'd check those when the boat was out of the water BEFORE the survey started?"

Sadly, this is not allowed[4]. You can only test these items AFTER the in-water sea trial has concluded.

When you agree to remove the boat from the water for these further checks, you're now committed to the boat at the agreed price unless you find something wrong that wasn't previously disclosed. Anything you discover during the sea trial is no longer a cause for rejection once you haul the boat out of the water.

Let's say that during the sea trial inspection, the surveyor noticed a minor water leak from the propellor shafts. Once the sea trial is completed and the boat is out of the water, that leak is no longer a reason to reject it, even if you find it's more severe than expected.

If the boat failed the sea trial, and you do decide to walk away, you'll now spend the next few weeks arguing over the return of the deposit. The seller will say you should contribute to the cost of the launch. You'll end up paying a lawyer to review the fine print to clarify for the seller that they agreed to pay the launch costs incurred, whether you purchased the boat or not.

All of this takes time, so perhaps you decided to move things along by going to sea trial with several boats in parallel. Good luck with that; remember, for each one, you're locking 10% of the purchase price down in a deposit.

---

3. Holes in the boat to let water in for various systems (like cooling your engine), hopefully in a controlled manner.

4. Strictly speaking... some sellers may agree, but it's not the standard in the contract.

Buying a boat works something like this[5] and turns out to be nothing like buying a house or a car. While it's actually more fun than it sounds, it's definitely NOT straightforward!

***

Putting these inherent difficulties in buying a boat aside, Covid-19 brought a raft of new challenges. It created an entirely new class of boat buyers like Karina and me. People using the enforced pause to rethink their lives and be intentional about how they want to invest their time and money.

Greece is home to many foreign-owned pleasure boats—British, French, German, and more. We're not the only people who realised Greece is a real boaters' paradise.

Covid-19 meant that owners couldn't just travel back to Greece due to restrictions in their home countries, in Greece, or just a general lack of flights. With the owners unable to be on-site, boats were even more poorly prepared than usual.

The pressures of the pandemic did create some buying opportunities. At least two boats we looked at were on the market because the owners were getting divorced and, therefore, selling assets. Boats are also a luxury item. When economies contract, they are quickly sold off.

On balance, though, the desire for people to reinvent their lives was winning out, and boats became a hot commodity. With factory shutdowns and increased demands, manufacturers reported that they'd sold out of their new stock several years in advance, which added even more pressure on the second-hand market we were interested in. As I write this, in 2023, boat demand remains very high.

When buying a second-hand boat, any significant transaction will likely involve a yacht broker who will guide you through the process. Typically, there is a broker representing the seller and another who represents the buyer.

With all this demand leading to more and more tire (fender) kickers for used boats, brokers were increasingly hard to find. They would rather not deal with people who weren't serious.

---

5. At least that's the way it works here in Greece and the broader Mediterranean. It's probably a different experience in the US, UK or Australia for example.

It's a catch-22. Serious buyers have a broker, so you would find it difficult to inspect a boat if you didn't have one. Of course, being unable to inspect a boat made it challenging to meet serious brokers...

To be clear, it's not meeting any old broker that's a problem; it's meeting the right one — the sort that will actually listen to you and help you, the novice boat buyer, negotiate this new and confusing world.

Unsurprisingly, buying a boat starts with looking at listings online. What's not immediately apparent is that this approach has three significant issues.

Issue number one is that there are two sorts of buyers of boats. New buyers like us and repeat buyers who already have a boat, a broker, and a relationship.

Repeat buyers are valuable to brokers, and they invest a lot of time in looking after them. This sort of buyer is also generally easier to service as they know what they want, and they tend to generate higher commissions because they are typically upgrading to bigger boats over time. They also don't need much education, having been through the process before.

Who wouldn't want a client who takes less work and pays more? The best brokers have a full client book and don't NEED to find more clients. They aren't looking or taking calls and essentially only accept new clients via word of mouth.

The best brokers all have an extensive word-of-mouth network. They know their client base and what they are interested in, and if a good listing comes onto the market, there's a good chance they already have someone in their network—either an existing client OR another trusted broker with a client who might be interested.

While you might think that advertising broadly is a good idea, the cost of prepping a boat for sale means that what you really want is a good lead on a solid buyer. Someone seriously interested, vs. a myriad of tire kickers who want to "get a feel" for the boat. If you can find a buyer within your network without advertising, it means fewer costs and better buyers.

Which leads to issue number two. The bad brokers, or the inexperienced ones who DON'T have a full client book, are building their business by advertising "anything".

That's right, numerous boat listings are fake.

A broker copies an existing listing and puts it up with their contact details, hoping to attract a potential client. Unfortunately, you'll waste a lot of time reaching out to these brokers only to find that the boat is suddenly "no longer available" or that they aren't the selling broker at all.

What's just happened is they've "wedged" themselves between you and the vendor, and now you have a buyer's broker you didn't want.

If the boat is no longer available (or was, in fact, never available), then, of course, it's at that point you'll find they have something else on their books that they think might meet your needs.

It won't.

The final issue is that, usually, it takes a long time for a boat to sell. To counter this, many vendors list their boats well before they are ready to sell on the theory that if it's going to take six months to move it, why not start that clock ticking now?

On two separate occasions, we found boats we wanted to view, only to be told by the vendor they had no interest in selling. They wanted to wait until after the season had completed, or they wanted an unreasonable amount of money this early in the process to give up their precious boat that they still had plans to use.

Despite these challenges, we lucked out early in the process and found ourselves an excellent broker.

***

Sometimes, even the best brokers get stuck with a terrible boat. Sotiris was no exception. He had helped an existing client move to a new, bigger boat, but their previous boat wasn't that marketable. Such is the relationship between a good broker and their existing clients. The client insisted that Sotiris should sell it – he wouldn't trust anyone else.

Which left Sotiris in a bind. He had a boat that was particularly unsuited for the Mediterranean (a small power cat), and no one in his network would be interested, so online it went.

All that was needed was some suitably naive buyers with no idea what they were looking for to come check it out. Did I mention we had no idea what we were doing and were looking for a boat?

Despite my earlier assertions that most boats you want to buy are stored up on the hard, in this particular instance, the boat was in the water at a marina and in Athens. Not a luxurious marina, but a big one. Alimos has been in the midst of upgrades for years, and it still has that "walking through a building site" feel I've come to associate with boat buying.

We arrived by tram from the city, excited to jump into inspecting our first boat right away. In Greece, though, it's the relationships that are key. Every meeting begins with a coffee. To our slight disappointment, we headed not to the dock but to the local cafe.

Sitting down, discussing our journey so far and our goals, Sotiris was immediately fascinated by our life's story. The idea of quitting our jobs at 50, moving to Greece and wanting to liveaboard a boat full time was surprisingly novel to him.

Most of his clients barely get to use their boats because they are too busy making more money. He took some time to wrap his head around the idea of simply saying "fuck you" and then running away to sea. Once he'd grasped it, though, he was immediately a big advocate.

It's a sentiment we've experienced many times now. Most people can't quite understand how they might make the same moves, either because they don't have the resources or, frankly, don't have the same tolerance for risk-taking that we do.

Even if they can't make that choice for themselves, most people tend to be advocates for the choices we've made. Even if it's so that they can watch the disaster unfold; after all, while you may not be willing to blow your own life up, there's an attraction in watching someone else actively throw away everything they've worked hard to achieve so far to pursue a crazy dream.

When we finally left the cafe to go visit the boat, we were immediately disappointed. It was too small, crowded, out of date and, as we understood with Sotiris' guidance, very poorly suited for the cruising we wanted to do.

From a performance perspective, it wasn't suited to the Aegean Sea and the strong winds called the Meltemi that blow during summer. And as a liveaboard option, while we thought a catamaran might have more living space, it was quickly apparent that this one did not. With the cabins crammed into the small hulls on either side, there wasn't a big enough bed for both of us.

Nowadays, we can assess that from photos without visiting, but that's the challenge of being a complete novice. You don't have a basis for comparison.

"I think I might have something that suits you better", says Sotiris. "Have you got time now?"

He called the owner and arranged the visit as we drove to the storage yard in the hills above Athens. Now, this was boat buying as we have become accustomed to it! A dusty, windy boatyard, a boat stored on the hard with tarpaulins flapping in the wind and a

"Filipino"[6] desperately hosing down the outside of the boat in a half-hearted attempt to clean it ready for our visit.

The boat was more to our style, but we weren't fans of the open targa-style cockpit (where 50% of the living space is permanently opened to the outside at the rear). It would be a great summer cruising boat, but it was too exposed for the true year-round liveaboard we were after. Still, we learnt a lot. We liked many aspects, including the styling, the room around the bed in the main cabin and the highly efficient pod drive engines.

During that afternoon, we got to know Sotiris better, and it was clear that the gears were turning in his mind. Like most Greeks we've met, he is incredibly generous with his time once you get to know him. It's the challenge of doing business here. Businesses are driven by relationships, which take time to maintain, so of course, if you have no relationship, you get given no time.

We spent much time together that afternoon over coffee and driving up into the hills. We spoke a lot about our vision of the lifestyle we wanted to achieve and shared our backgrounds and our love for exploring the world.

By the end of the afternoon, Sotiris understood that we weren't just tire kickers. We genuinely wanted to buy a boat, and we wanted to do it soon. I think he could also see how inexperienced we were at the process, and he was genuinely worried that we had no idea how to go about it.

By the time he dropped us off at our final destination, he'd reached a decision. "I'm going to help you buy a boat."

We'd continued to march forward, and we'd found the right person to guide us on the next steps of the journey. We didn't realise at the time just how fortunate we were to have Sotiris working on our behalf. Only later would we appreciate just how far out of the league of his typical clients we really were.

Which is all part of the glorious nature of doing business in Greece. Money matters, but relationships matter more. We'd made a good impression, liked each other, and were serious. That was important and more than enough for Sotiris to add us as his first new boat-buying client in years.

---

6. We have no idea if he was Filipino or not. The association between Filipinas and domestic or manual work is so strong in Greece that a Greek dictionary published in 1998 even defined "Filippineza", a term which literally means Filipina, to be "a domestic worker from the Philippines or a person who performs non-essential auxiliary tasks". Considered inappropriate now, the term is still common, especially amongst older people who will have a "Filipino" to crew and clean their boat.

Five

Compromise

"I do not know what 'moss' stands for in the proverb, but if it stood for useful knowledge... I gathered more moss by rolling than I ever did at school." — Ernest Shackleton

You don't know what you don't know. While we were aware that we had a lot to learn, we also knew less about what we were trying to do than we expected. It's a common theme in tech startups. Founders will often express some variant of "If I knew how hard it was going to be, I never would have started".

Speaking with others who've bought a boat since, the sentiment around boat buying is very similar. All you can do is try to solve the next problem before you and be grateful that you're blissfully unaware of the ten more complicated steps to follow.

I'm sure we've all expressed strong opinions that, lacking experience, come back to haunt us. For us, during those first few months, it was the answer to the question, "Why did you move to Greece?"

With no better idea, when asked why we had moved, we always answered confidently, "We're here to buy a boat and liveaboard. We should be on the water by Christmas."

Yeah... no. Sotiris would simply roll his eyes and say, "We'll see".

Now, with two winters in Greece under our belt, we would never try to stay on the boat in the way we originally intended beyond December. Already by November, the winds are unsettled and changing quickly. The temperature is cool; crossings are difficult and uncomfortable. You constantly fight to move from safe harbour to safe harbour, and when you do get where you're going, everything, especially on the islands, is closed anyway.

If someone were to say to me now, "We want to cruise in Greece through December," I'd understand that they were either highly experienced or, more likely, they had no idea what they were talking about.

Regardless, I'd be politely discouraging them from what I now know to be a clearly ridiculous idea. Almost certainly, that advice would be brushed aside.

Plenty of people tried to tell us cruising through December was pointless. But despite the wealth of knowledge we were building through research online and the people we were meeting, it was our goal, and we were determined to achieve it.

Sometimes, things really do have to be experienced to be understood.

An excellent example is the Meltemi winds that consistently appear in parts of Greece during summer. At their simplest, they are easy to describe. They are strong, cool, dry seasonal winds that occur throughout the Aegean Sea in summer. They can be intense – over 30 knots (Beaufort 7) — and last several days.

While accurate, this description understates their soul-searing constant pressure. The winds hold steady for days or weeks, grating at you like fine sandpaper, gradually driving you to the edge of insanity.

Residents often welcome the Meltemi as a pleasant relief from the heat, but the wind is generally unwanted by tourists as beaches turn into sandstorms. Previously calm seas become rough and even dangerous on the north side of the islands, particularly in the popular Cyclades. In extreme cases, ferries and flights between islands are cancelled.

For experienced sailors and, more specifically, sailboats, the Meltemi conditions can offer an exhilarating thrill that promises "real" sailing. They are usually best avoided by novice skippers on charter boats. During the Meltemi, most boats will remain tied up in port or head west into the Saronic Gulf, away from the worst of the wind.

Aristotle even wrote about them in his book, Meteoroligica, which dates to the late 4th Century BCE. At the time, they were called the Etesian Winds, which in Ancient Greek means annual. The Meltemi has been around for a while. So when experienced people warn you about them, perhaps you should pay attention; they've lived through them and understand what they are about.

Yet, every season, novice sailors have poor experiences sailing in Greece because they believe that "surely the Meltemi can't be that bad?"

Even if you grasp the mechanics of the Meltemi winds and treat them with respect, you haven't started to understand them until you appreciate the deep hold they have on the psyche of Greek sailors.

On more than one occasion, we looked at a boat that seemed fine to us, but when we discussed in further detail what we were trying to achieve, someone (usually Sotiris) would ask, "Yes, but what about the Meltemi?"

Any other Greek person present would nod as if this were a complete sentence in its own right. The boat in question would be dismissed immediately out of hand, leaving us to wonder what had just happened.

For someone who's lived in Greece, who has grown up and been moulded by the Meltemi over endless summers, this is a profoundly insightful observation.

It raises questions about the boat's suitability for the purpose you intend to use it for. It implies that for three months of the year in this boat, you'll have to seek shelter, hiding from the wind and the waves and only venturing out for short periods.

In this boat, you won't exactly be a liveaboard, cruising the ocean waves. Instead, you'll resemble a hermit crab, popping your head out briefly to quickly pull it in again. No further explanation is needed. "What about the Meltemi?" is a self-evident rhetorical question providing all the necessary context.

Its counterpart, the simple statement "is good for the Meltemi," accompanied by a brief head nod, says that this is a boat you can trust. It's capable of handling the conditions you'll experience and is the right boat for what you're setting out to do.

Of course, to novice sailors, which firmly includes us... we hear about the Meltemi and think, "Surely it can't be that bad. It's just weather."

And this is only one of the many examples of what you need to learn. Successfully buying the right boat is more than just the raw numbers. It's a strange combination of emotion, experience, and a lot of luck. It requires learning a whole new language and, indeed, an entirely new culture.

***

What Sotiris knew that we failed to appreciate is that boat buying takes time. Beyond simply finding the perfect boat, a seemingly endless number of steps must be completed.

He knew it was improbable that any significant boat sale could be completed within a few months. Given that we were already approaching mid-September, he knew there was no way we would be living aboard by December.

The idea that we could find the right boat, agree on a price, negotiate the contract and then deal with the legal transfer (which can be very complex depending on where the boat is registered and the new country you want to register it in) was naive at best, especially with the added complexities of a global pandemic. We were eternally optimistic in a way we had no right to be.

Yet here's the thing: he was willing to try. Our experience of working with Greek people is that while they may firmly believe you're insane if they like you, it won't stop them trying to help you succeed.

I'm convinced that, at heart, all Greeks are a little crazy, too. It's a quality I've come to appreciate. Business in Greece is about relationships. Once someone is on board, they are enthusiastically on board, regardless of where the crazy Australians choose to take them.

We'd learn this lesson soon enough that finding the right boat takes time. Still, in those early few weeks, we were like toddlers, determined to stick our fingers into every power socket without understanding the risks involved or how electricity works.

Sotiris tried his best to steer us away from the worst disasters as we enthusiastically kept putting forward boat after boat we found online. It didn't matter how poorly suited it was because we were desperate to find something and to be out there on the water, REAL SOON.

While he saved us from our worst impulses, eventually, the guard rails came down, and we were set footloose and free into the world to view boats on our own. I suspect he regretted the time we flew to Samos to inspect a boat without him.

It started well. After the heat and chaos of Athens, Samos was a wonderful place to be. One of the defining things for us about travelling in Greece is that you can't help but trip over history. Samos is no exception. The port we were visiting, Pythagoria, was, unsurprisingly, the birthplace of Pythagoras[1] . A statue of him, holding a right-angle triangle, sits at one end of the town quay, watching over the ships coming and going.

The island is green and luxurious, the people friendly, it has some fascinating ruins, and several great beaches. All of these things, in combination, held a blow torch to our desire to get out there on our own boat and start exploring.

---

1. c. 570 BC. Mathematician and philosopher a.k.a that triangle theory guy.

For the first time since arriving in Greece, Karina and I were in an island port and could see the dream laid out before us. Pythagoria was full of liveaboards lining the town quay stern-to, even this late in the season. A stern-to, or Med mooring, is a common feature of town quays throughout Greece. When mooring stern-to, you drop the anchor some distance in front of where you want to dock and then reverse the boat to the quay, tying the ropes to the shore from the stern. It allows many boats to pack in like sardines. Where one boat might be able to tie alongside, you can instead fit 2–3 boats stern-to.

Whenever we could catch someone's eye, we'd talk to them about their journey and plans for the future. "We're here to buy a boat", we'd say confidently when they asked us what we were up to in return.

There was so little we understood about their life and why these people were even here. Two days after we arrived, they all suddenly left.

"We were surprised the boats all disappeared," we told Christos, the agent we met in Samos.

"Ahh, the Meltemi just ended." Enough said.

Christos was a gruff but helpful man. He had little skin in the game, not the broker, but acting on behalf of a more prominent agent based out of Corfu. While he would make some money if the boat sold, his involvement was more as a favour than a primary source of income.

Born and bred in Pythagoria, he told tales of life on the islands and recommended places to visit. He kindly drove us to the top of the nearby hill, where we could see a church inside a cave. While there, he shared memories of sheltering inside as a child to hide from a potential Turk incursion when the Turks invaded Cyprus in 1974.

Seen through his eyes, Samos was more than just another Greek island; it began to take on mythic qualities as the only place to be. There was, according to Christos, nowhere quite like it.

This is what we wanted to experience. The raw enthusiasm for his homeland fanned our desire to get out there and discover. What better life than to explore island after island, to spend time with locals and uncover the hidden secrets? We were already excited about the journey ahead of us, and now, with the dream come to life as we sat on the quay in Samos, it couldn't happen fast enough. And then we went to see the boats.

The first was immediately unavailable. Between the time we left Athens and arrived in Samos, the owner decided he would use the weather window to move his boat to another island despite our appointment. Christos suggested we could take a ferry to catch up to it, but the connections with our existing flight times wouldn't work. With no desire to chase the boat around the Aegean and no guarantee the owner would wait, we quickly crossed it off our list.

For the second boat, Christos drove us out to the nearby marina to view a Beneteau Swift Trawler 44. Despite being a popular production boat, it didn't take long to decide that it wouldn't suit us. The access to the flybridge was up a ladder, which was no good for our dog Rosie, and the typical three-cabin layout in a boat that size made it feel cramped overall.

Realising quickly that we weren't giving off positive vibes, Christos leapt into action. "You know, if you don't like this boat – if you want to see one with a large main cabin — I can show you another one here. Should I call the owner and see if I can take you aboard?"

It's at this point that Sotiris would regret leaving us unattended.

"Yes, please! We're always happy to see more boats."

The boat in question was a 60 ft (ca. 18 m) Fairline. It's hard to appreciate just how big that is, but from the moment we boarded, all we could see was space. Spread over two levels, it was close to an extra 50 square metres on the Beneteau Swift Trawler we'd just left.

Going from small to big is never the right direction for viewing boats. Forget about the clothes strewn on the floor and the baby's high chair still attached to the main table. All we could see was that here was a boat that we could stretch out on.

Logically, we knew that only considering the space was a bad idea, but emotionally, we'd already fallen hard for the owner's cabin. Not only was there room to swing a proverbial cat, but probably a horse as well. This was a boat we could live on.

One of the hardest things about making a purchase you care about is remaining un-emotional, especially with Christos enthusiastically congratulating you on your questions and taste.

While the size was generous, there were a few issues, but for every problem, Christos had an answer... "yes, the teak needs some work, but we estimated for another potential buyer, €50,000 to fix everything".

"Does that include the headlining[2]?" I was keen to show off my growing boat vocabulary.

---

2. The fabric that covers the interior of the ceiling is called headlining. As it ages, the glue deteriorates and it sags, so it needs to be replaced. It serves no purpose but decoration, and to fall down at inconvenient times.

"Yes, yes, of course, everything. She is in perfect condition. It's so sad; the owners left due to Covid-19, and now they are getting divorced, but it's a wonderful boat. Good for the Meltemi."

By the time we returned to Sotiris back in Athens, we'd agreed to move to sea trial. With hindsight, it was more than just the boat. We'd also fallen a little too in love with Samos. There was no time to waste; we needed a boat, and we needed to get out there NOW. This one would do.

"You what?!" Sotiris was clearly unhappy with this news.

"It's amazing! It's got so much room," we bashfully pointed out. It was painfully clear that 'room' wasn't precisely hitting with Sotiris as the selling point it initially appeared to us.

"You're going to need a crew for that thing. Have you ever driven a boat that large?"

We get it now. It's not the going in boats that's the problem — it's the stopping. Any idiot can jump into a boat, punch the throttles and manoeuvre it forward. But, when you have to park it between two other boats in a tight port, with the wind blowing 20 knots across the beam, that's a different story.

Still, we didn't get this far without a high degree of confidence... "I'm sure we can learn."

"Well, what about the condition?" If we weren't going to be talked out of it, Sotiris was at least there to focus on the practical aspects of the transaction.

"We've been told it only needs about €50k to make it perfect, but even if it's €60k or €70k, it's still a bargain!" We felt convinced that Brexit and Covid-19 were working in our favour. While tragic for them, we thought the owners' impending divorce had opened an opportunity right before us.

Sotiris obviously thought we were crazy to consider it, but, as we established earlier, crazy has never stopped a Greek.

"I'll help you," he said, "but promise me that if the purchase goes through, you'll hire a captain for the first month or two while you learn." He finished up with, "I'm going to make sure the contract is good, so we can get your money back later..."

Two weeks after this conversation and roughly €5,000 in travel, accommodation, and costs associated with bringing Sotiris, our surveyor and an engine mechanic, to Samos with us, we walked away from the boat before the sea trial even commenced.

The two local mechanics on site were unable even to start the engines. Our mechanic, an authorised MAN engineer, stepped in, and with his assistance and several hours, they managed to get the boat underway. We'd already walked away from the deal, but they invited us for a brief cruise while they tested the boat now that it had finally started. Further issues arose on the short trial when the turbo wouldn't activate, leaving it unable to go faster than a slow idle. While it might have only needed €50k in cosmetics (and frankly, it needed more), this boat was a disaster mechanically.

Later, over a beer, our mechanic told us that the boat had also clearly been run onto the rocks at least once.

"The engines were showing a fatal shutdown error, and both engines failed at the same time – for that to happen – both engines to fail at the same time, it was likely flooded. Also, they replaced one of the engine mounts and only one of the alternators, both on the starboard side. You'd normally do those at the same time. Only replacing them on starboard suggests it had taken on salt water and was lying on that side, which damaged things."

While it was an expensive lesson, we're thankful it only cost us €5,000 to walk away. If we'd bought it, we'd have spent much more than we ever intended on making it sound. With the benefit of more experience and hindsight, we're incredibly thankful that the purchase fell through.

We learnt many valuable things, but two stick out. One, never pick a boat because of how much you like the main cabin and two, we were incredibly fortunate to have Sotiris on our side.

After the sea trial, he dragged out the contract, disappeared into the office with the other broker, and two days later, we had our deposit back.

Strangely, after Samos, Sotiris never let us go and inspect a boat unattended again.

***

With each boat we inspected, we gained more experience about what we really wanted. A vague list of "not a sailboat" (a point Karina wasn't willing to compromise on) and "a main cabin with a walk-around bed" became increasingly more specific. Gradually, it narrowed further into brands we liked and styling that we didn't. Engines and fuel consumption (the lower, the better) went up the list, and even the Meltemi performance became a concern.

Sotiris found another Sealine, similar to the one we first saw when we met him, but this time without the targa back. It was located in a small town called Kilada on the Peloponnese, a 2.5-hour drive from Athens.

A small fishing village, Kilada has gained prominence in the cruising community due to two key factors. One is that it's on a bay with year-round protection from winds and is a safe place to leave a boat. The second is the large boatyard, which stores around 350 boats and has run as a family-operated business since 1965. Like many Greek villages, it's a hodgepodge of tidy, clean and upgraded facilities to attract tourists surrounded by the detritus of a working fishing village. Newly paved sidewalks pass trendy cafes, which then dead end into unfinished dirt areas along the shore, full of weeds, rubbish and half-salvaged boats.

The boatyard, however, is very professionally run and full of fancy boats all on hard stand. As we walked through the yard to inspect the Sealine, gawking at the other yachts on the way, we passed an ungainly-looking trawler-style boat. It had an info sheet warped from moisture with ink running down the page, stapled to a display board underneath the bow. At the top of the page was a big headline, "For Sale," and a series of photos and a link to a website below.

I browsed the specs and mentioned to Karina that this one looked interesting.

She glanced at the photos and dismissed it immediately, "too much wood, too old-fashioned".

Sotiris just smiled and took several photos of the brochure, then off we walked to inspect the boat we were there to see.

Little did we know it then, but that ugly trawler with "too much wood" was the boat we'd eventually buy. It would take us four more months to realise we'd just seen the one. Ironically, the initial dream of purchasing and moving aboard by December might have come true, but we still had to work through and cross off a long list of other options first to discover more about what we really needed.

Not all boats were dismissed because they were disasters, far from it. One growing frustration was that we were starting to narrow in on the sort of boat we liked, but we could never complete an offer for various reasons.

The Sealine we went to see in Kilada was a great choice. It was in excellent condition, modern and had a mid-ship main cabin. With pod drives, it was also highly economical. We quickly made an offer to try to get it to sea trial.

After several rounds of negotiation, it soon became apparent that while the husband wanted to sell and move on to a bigger boat, he hadn't mentioned this to his wife. As part owner, she refused when she was required to put her signature on the offer.

Then, the Covid-19 lockdown started again in Greece, which further hampered our ability to move around and slowed boat visits even further. But we kept hunting online, researching and visiting what we could.

We found an Azimut Magellano, a beautiful Italian-styled boat that checked most of the boxes but pushed our budget to the limit. The deal failed when it was clear the original purchase was mired in tax problems, and it was unclear if the VAT had ever been paid.

Convinced that an Azimut Magellano was the one, we tracked down the same model in Montenegro. The owner refused to sign a standard agreement to allow a sea trial and added a series of clauses that caused concern. A big worry was that he needed us to put down almost 50% of the purchase price before the sea trial so that he could pay out his lease. We walked away.

In Italy, we found an Aicon 56 that looked interesting and paid a local surveyor to do a pre-sales inspection. It wasn't possible to travel to Italy due to lockdowns. Still, given we were familiar with the model after viewing one on the hard in Athens, we felt a professional opinion on quality would be enough.

Everything looked great, except the owner could not produce the sales receipts. These are critical to prove that a) he owned the boat and b) that the tax (VAT) had been paid. Without this, according to our lawyer, there was every chance we'd have to pay VAT again when moving the boat from Italy to Greece. We decided to keep waiting on the documentation but would also move forward with inspecting other boats.

By early February 2021, we'd reached an impasse. There were literally no further boats available for sale at that moment in the Mediterranean that met the strict set of criteria we'd come up with. Something had to change.

To paraphrase Shackleton, we'd gathered more moss by rolling than we would have done standing still. With our hard-earned (and sometimes costly) experience, it was time to rethink what we needed. We had some challenging discussions and made hard decisions, forcing the new list of priorities to come together quickly.

If we were going to buy a power boat, it was clear that fuel consumption was critical from an environmental and cost perspective. We also wanted to have the fuel capacity and range to be able to explore, which meant we had to prioritise trawler (or displacement[3]) style boats.

Our budget also needed to go up. We now had more realistic expectations about what things would cost, and increasing the amount we were willing to spend would let a few more boats creep into consideration.

Styling, to Karina's disappointment, went down the list. There's been a fundamental shift in boat design philosophy since roughly 2012, with more modern, lighter and open interiors hitting the market, replacing the older, heavily wooded teak and oak-style interiors. Unfortunately, a newer boat was pushing our budget too far. We'd almost certainly be buying a slightly older, cheaper boat and, therefore, have to accept the accompanying design philosophy.

Eventually, we settled on an extensive list of about 20 items; some must-haves, others nice to have. We reviewed the available yachts in the Mediterranean again, then force-ranked them according to the criteria we'd developed. By the end of the day, we'd come up with a new list of 10 boats. The third on the list was an Adagio LBC Sundeck Trawler 44, currently stored on the hard in Kilada.

Within a week, the first two on the list had been ruled out.

The first was the Italian Aicon we were already looking at with the missing VAT paperwork. As we continued to insist on the seller producing the correct documentation to proceed, they "miraculously" found another buyer[4], and we walked away.

The second boat was a Selene 49, located in Cyprus. They already had an interested buyer, and the seller didn't want to negotiate, so it ended up outside our price range.

On to number three! The ugly duckling of a boat we didn't even look at in October was the one. With the right combination of features, she'd turned into a beautiful swan. Okay, maybe not quite that, but there was no doubt that the fuel efficiency, space and general level of options fitted to the boat made her a better-than-average choice for what we needed.

Sotiris, prescient as ever, was already a step ahead.

---

3. Without getting too technical, a displacement style boat will go far slowly, vs a planing style boat which will go fast, but burn huge amounts of fuel.

4. It's likely this other buyer never existed and was simply created to pressure us to close without the right documents. Two weeks later the other buyer "fell through" and the owner came back promising they might actually find the paperwork this time. We'd already moved on.

He'd already been in contact with the seller and had a detailed brochure ready to go. The boat was well-equipped and, on paper at least, well-maintained. They even had the original invoice showing VAT was paid. It was time to move to sea trial again.

***

One sunny afternoon in April, we headed back down to Kilada, an exciting escape from Athens and a lockdown that had restricted travel to all but essential activities — like boat buying. Seriously. With a piece of paper to say we were off to visit a boat we wanted to purchase, we could easily move about the country.

While lockdowns were ostensibly there to prevent the spread of Covid-19, there were sufficient loopholes to enable commerce to continue. Were you a tourist heading to a resort? Sure, you can move around. Wanted to spend money? No worries! Have you rented an Airbnb in the countryside to get out of the city? Go for it!

That last loophole was acceptable until March 2021, when they realised so many people were leaving the city for Airbnb's in the countryside that they explicitly closed it down. The point was that lockdown, while severe for most people, was less painful for those connected to economic activities.

After Athens, where the Covid-19 lockdowns were still quite severe, Kilada was a breath of fresh air... literally. No one was wearing masks that we could see. It felt like, at least in this small corner of the world, that Covid-19 had passed it by.

This was our third visit to Kilada, and, like many places in Greece, it grows on you. There's a rugged beauty in the desolate villages that's not always immediately apparent. Walking along the foreshore, we could see the boat already afloat and ready to go at the dock. This was a significant change from the Fairline we saw in Samos.

We soaked it all in, admiring how much different this boat looked in the water compared to when we last saw it on the hard. While you would be hard-pressed to describe this particular boat as beautiful, there was a refined grace now seeing it in its natural element. The turtles were frolicking in the bay, swimming around while we stood back, waiting for Sotiris to drive separately from Athens. After so many failed attempts, the feeling was building that we might have found the right one.

Once Sotiris arrived, we met the owners, an older French couple, who were there already and excited to show us around. With Sotiris and our surveyor, we crawled over every part of the boat we could reach and poked, prodded and tested every system we could find.

There were a few quirks, like the fuse for the anchor windlass buried deep underneath the guest bed, but overall, everything looked in good shape, and there were no major red flags. With several boat inspections under our belt now, we'd come to accept that not everything is perfect. It's about working out what's critical and what's just a part of the personality of your boat.

The main cabin was huge, a win right out of the gate and for its length, the layout was very roomy, but there were also compromises. The kitchen was a "down galley", sitting forward of the salon and down three steep steps, not open to the cockpit and entertaining as is more common in modern trawler designs.

Probably most damning in our eyes was the interior wooden styling in full teak. Some people prefer this more classic, old-fashioned feel, but we find it overwhelming in contrast to our minimalist style. It wasn't helped with the carpets and curtains, both dark and heavy, but those at least could be easily remedied.

The best news was that this boat was a true Mediterranean explorer. The French owners had already travelled extensively through the canals of France and into Germany, then to the Mediterranean and Spain, Italy, and finally, five seasons in Greece.

We knew that with this boat, we had a reliable base for our explorations with the room we needed. Economically, she sipped fuel; compared to other power boats of a similar size, we would consume roughly 20% of their fuel, with the trade-off that we would travel much slower.

For the first time, we not only completed an initial survey but also gave the go-ahead to take the boat to sea trial. We set out from the harbour for a cruise, respecting the Covid-19 restrictions, which allowed us to travel only to the entrance to the bay but not further. The mechanic and the surveyor were both impressed. The few things that required attention were minor and well within expectations.

Our surveyor, a taciturn British-Greek man of few words who also travelled with us to Samos, said, "I'd buy it. I was worried about that Fairline in Samos, but this is the right first boat for you."

It's more words than he'd spoken in one go before, and it sealed the deal for us.

As we returned to the dock, we looked up at the current owners, sitting together quietly at the helm, the wife resting her head on her husband's shoulder. You could tell they were soaking up the atmosphere of what we all suspected would be their last journey on their boat.

Both Karina and I shed a quiet tear at the bitter-sweet moment. It was clear how much this boat meant to them. It felt like we were taking over a member of their family. But we were also nursing a quiet excitement. After all this time, we'd found the one and couldn't wait to take the next steps!

Six

Reality

"The sea finds out everything you did wrong." — Francis Stokes

If there's one lesson that travel and boat life has taught us, it's that things rarely run to plan. It's been a tough lesson to learn. Having finally found "the one", and with the challenges of the boat hunt now behind us, we assumed we'd move rapidly from the sea trial to the final documentation and sale. Experience should have taught us that this would not be the case. There were more than a few curveballs to come.

And really, why wouldn't there be?

We were about to spend a couple of hundred thousand euros on a boat purchased in Greece, registered under a French Flag. It was being bought from a French couple while transferring the ownership to a Dutch person (Karina). Then, to top it off, cancelling the French registration and re-registering (flagging) it in Poland.

More than just buying a boat, you're now talking about a somewhat complex international transaction with several moving parts to be taken care of. All occurring in the middle of a global pandemic and continuing lockdowns.

After the sea trial, there was a flurry of paperwork. A seemingly endless filling of boat details, copying them from one piece of paper to a new piece of paper. All to request action from various government departments. While the world at large may be moving to digital, the world of boats has remained firmly in the analogue.

It was at this point our lawyer noticed a missing zero.

"The starboard engine serial number has one less zero than the port one."

Both engines have serial numbers with leading zeros, but the starboard engine had only five instead of six.

"And it's written on the contract and in the 'Fiche de Navigre[1]' with five zeros, but this original bill of sale shows the engine number with six zeros", he mused. "Do you know anything about this?"

Several emails went back and forth between the lawyer and the sellers, including a visible inspection of the engines, and we received the bad news. This was going to be a problem. Our appreciation of the value the lawyer was bringing went up.

When the boat was first registered in France, someone had misplaced a zero when writing the starboard engine number on a form. The physical engine numbers no longer exactly matched the registration on file. Despite the obvious error, it could create issues with the new registration in Poland. Sure, you could TRY to explain it was a simple error, but it would be better to rectify it now.

The correct way to fix it was for the previous owners to file an amendment with the French authorities, formally updating the paperwork. This way, when we received the official notice of de-registration, the engine serial numbers would correctly match the original bill of sale.

While it is pedantic, it's unfortunately essential. Like with a car, the body and the engine numbers must match the registration; otherwise, the authorities might think there's something amiss.

Things rapidly went downhill when the original registration document, which had to be couriered from the boat back to France for amendment, was lost. It became detached from the courier's tracking information between Greece and France. For three weeks, the document showed as sitting in the courier's office near the boatyard, nowhere to be found.

Where we'd estimated roughly two weeks for the de-flagging in France, it was already a month later, and we were still waiting for the engine serial numbers to match the actual registration document.

Looking back, it seems trivial, but at the time, nine months into the boat-buying process, we felt we were getting further stonewalled by the day. We'd missed our initial "by Christmas" deadline and were now well into April without further progress. It felt like we were also in danger of missing our first summer.

---

1. The French official boat registration - like registering your car.

Finally, it was resolved in the most traditional of ways—someone who knew someone called in a favour and made something happen.

The agent that initially sold the boat to the French owners stepped in at their request. He went to the registration offices, and the next day, a replacement registration certificate was issued. The incorrect serial number was magically corrected.

We never found out if the original certificate had finally been delivered for amendment or a new one conjured out of a bureaucratic black box. We didn't care. With the corrected registration certificate now in hand, we could finally complete the sale, and, as the new owners, we requested the de-registration of the boat.

Three weeks later, we received an email from our lawyer. The de-registration in France was completed, and now it was on to the new official registration in Poland.

Unlike Greece and France, Poland appeared less interested in the bureaucracy and more interested in the money; within two weeks, we had the official Polish registration, and the process was complete. Our boat now had her new official name, *Matilda* and with the correct registration, we could finalise our insurance, put her back into the water and start to sail the seas.

If there's a lesson in all this, you might think it's that optimism is not a good trait for a boat owner. And you'd be partially correct. But in reality, a boat owner without a healthy dose of optimism would never get anything done. If you expect things to go wrong, you'll never leave port. Optimism is essential, but a more challenging trait to cultivate is the healthy acceptance of reality. Sometimes, things just are the way they are.

***

Finally, we could make moves to begin our new life on the sea. Within a day, we'd left Athens to travel to Kilada and move aboard. *Matilda* was ours. It's tempting to think that at that point, we motored off into the sunset and started our life aboard. Reality had other plans.

I had the correct qualifications and certificates, if not all the experience at the time, to charter and captain a sailing boat in most places worldwide. But for a power boat like *Matilda*, the Greek authorities required the skipper to hold a separate motorboat license.

While the requirement initially frustrated us, we approached it with a positive mindset. More training has to be a good thing, right? It was also an excellent opportunity for

Karina to get some training and gain the technical skills and certificates required to skipper *Matilda* too.

At face value, the insistence on a motorboat license makes sense, but as we discovered when we undertook the training, there is a significant mismatch between the actual skills you practice and those you need.

At least the training schools are common. As you travel around Greece and its harbours, a common sight is a small 4 – 6 metre (ca. 13–20 ft) open power boat with an outboard motor and "Training Boat" written on the side. In busier ports, there might be three or four of them active at the same time.

They circle the harbour, they pull up alongside large yachts, they reverse, they... well, they practise all the basic, valuable skills a skipper of a small boat with a big outboard motor would need. Which is probably the typical boat that the people taking the course will use. A small boat for day trips to an island or fishing. Something you can bring with you on a trailer when you go on holiday.

It's also the same boat you do your practical test in. Like a driving test, you sit down with an assessor (the port police, in this instance), who watches you execute the skills you've been practising and gives you a pass or fail grade. You're now a registered motorboat captain!

What doesn't make sense is that the license you have just acquired allows you to skipper any motorboat up to a 25-metre (ca. 82 ft) yacht. If you're not that familiar with boats, it may be hard to appreciate the lunacy of this.

There's a big difference between driving a small 6 metre (ca. 13-foot) boat with an outboard and piloting *Matilda*, with twin inline diesels, 240HP on each engine, 13 metres (ca. 43 ft) long and weighing around 16 tonnes, which is entirely different again from a 20 metre (ca. 65 foot) yacht burning 300L an hour and travelling at 40 knots up on the plane[2].

Imagine learning to drive in a tiny go-kart and having demonstrated you can successfully drive it around your local go-kart track, being immediately given the keys to drive a manual tractor and a performance sports car on the open road.

---

2. To go fast, you spend a lot of fuel, but you push the boat out of the water and plane, or glide, across the top.

Not that the practical skills were wasted. Time on the water and familiarity with boats is always a good thing. It's just that they weren't the specific practical skills we needed to operate *Matilda*.

In addition to the skills, we had to sit a theory exam. This was much more useful. When it comes to piloting boats, apart from a few minor local quirks between countries, most of the rules are universal. Referred to as "COLREGs[3]", these are set by various international treaties and govern boats moving back and forth worldwide.

The local quirks are, for the most part, also helpful to know. For example, how close can you anchor to a beach with swimmers in Greece? Occasionally though, the theory questions were obscure.

The term "en plo" (transliterated from Greek) means "underway". Understanding what "underway" is as a concept does have merit and is defined in the COLREGs. But do you need to know what it's called in Greek? Not so much.

With one specific exception. We've since found many Greek ports have a local restaurant called "en plo". Now we know exactly what that refers to.

Another quirk was learning the names of the winds. It does have cultural relevance as these names have existed for thousands of years. But except for the Meltemi, for all practical purposes, we've never heard them referred to since. Even the official Greek Coast Guard announcements for the weather on the radio give the forecast wind as compass directions and strength (NW, 4 Beaufort).

While the theory covered was extensive, the quality of the actual training materials let it down. We were handed a set of seven multiple-choice tests, poorly translated to English, an answer sheet, and a straightforward instruction.

"Answer these until you get them all right."

Which we did, but there are mysteries hidden in the details we could never understand. For example. "What is the correct amount of chain to anchor in 5 metres (ca. 16 ft) of water?" I've been taught a simple formula in previous theory tests, like "5 times depth". As a multiple choice answer, there was a 25 metre (ca. 82 ft) option. This turns out to be the correct answer, but there was no explanation of the theory or a rule provided to justify that amount.

Still, given that I had the correct answer, clearly, I knew the rule already. Or did I?

---

3. The Convention on the International Regulations for Preventing Collisions at Sea. Which updated the previously named Collision Regulations, hence COLREGs.

At 10 metres (ca. 33 ft) of depth, the correct multiple choice answer for the amount of chain was now 45 metres (ca. 148 ft) of chain. No one ever bothered to explain why, in Greece, they would expect 45 metres of chain in 10 metres of water instead of the 50 metres (ca. 164 ft) that the 5:1 rule would predict. We rote learnt the answer and moved on.

The test itself was conducted in very controlled conditions. The Coast Guard pride themselves on producing a test that's taken fairly. Each test is randomised and different for every batch of students, with one fatal flaw. While the test itself is randomly generated, the pool of questions used to create them matches precisely the questions on the seven sample tests we had just rote learnt the answers to.

To make everything just that bit more challenging, we also needed to conduct the test in Greek. Remember, we'd learnt the answers to the questions in poorly translated English. As part of the training, we were provided with a translator who also sat beside us for the duration of the test. A port police officer was also seated opposite our table, observing us to ensure that we weren't colluding with our translator and that the student was completing the test.

Ioanna, our translator, was a friendly Greek woman who, like many people we met, was fascinated with our goal of living aboard. We'd already been working with her for several weeks on the training boats, as she was also the translator between us and our instructor.

Entering the hall for the test, she says to me, "When we sit down, make sure you sit close to me."

My immediate assumption was that she intended this as a courtesy to the other 30 students taking the test. No doubt, she didn't want them disturbed by her reading the questions aloud. Nope. I sat close to her, near enough that she could easily whisper to me.

"Closer", she hissed, then grabbed my leg and pulled it by the knee until it touched hers.

Ok. This wasn't quite what I was expecting. With the test beginning, there was no further time to ask questions. Then, all of a sudden, her intent became painfully clear.

She translated the first question for me. "Question one. How much chain do you need in 5 metres of water? Is it a) 20 metres, b) 30 metres, c) 25 metres, Ioanna violently steps on my toe"... or d) 40 metres?"

The reality was we didn't need the extra assistance, as we'd both studied diligently. We were confident that we would have aced it regardless. But in true Greek fashion, our instructors had promised we would pass. They were committed to us succeeding, boots and all, even if it did mean crushing our toes for every correct answer, all within two metres of the police invigilator.

After the theory section, we headed to the port with the other students to wait for the results. Once confirmation was received that the theory had been passed, then the practical session would start. We would take the boat we'd been training in and manoeuvre it under the supervision of a port policeman.

As Karina and I were sitting in the shade waiting for the results, I noticed all the other students with lengths of rope practising tying knots.

"Ahhh, Ioanna..." I asked. "Are we supposed to know how to tie those?"

"Yes, of course! Dimitris (our instructor) showed you. You have to demonstrate them to the port policeman."

"No, he didn't..."

"..."

A brief panic ensued as Ioanna found Dimitris (in true Greek fashion, drinking a Freddo Cappuccino with his other instructor mates) and dragged him back to us. An animated conversation ensued in Greek, the gist of which seemed to be Dimitris insisting he'd already shown us the knots.

"He definitely didn't," said Karina.

A series of shrugs from Dimitris and two pieces of rope were quickly procured. We were instructed in the four basic knots they wanted to see and, importantly, the Greek names for them.

Our bruised toes might yet be in vain. Without being able to demonstrate the knots, we would fail the practical.

Fortunately, I already knew the knots demonstrated; I just needed to know how they named them to produce them when asked. Karina, however, had the more challenging task of learning and practising them all only 10 minutes before she started her practical test.

Fifteen minutes later, it was all over. A quick turn around the port, a brief motor in reverse and several theory questions later, I was signed off as a Powerboat Captain by the port police.

Karina also passed with flying colours despite having a much more rigorous and involved assessment. Her practical test finally ended when Dimitris and Ioanna argued with the assessor, telling him he was being excessive and only grilling her because she was a woman.

This was all yet to come, however. At the time we moved aboard *Matilda*, we weren't yet allowed to pilot her.

Covid-19 lockdowns meant that all the training schools had been closed and were now just reopening. If we were going to put *Matilda* in the water and liveaboard, we had to hire a captain to help us move the boat on launch day.

***

Matilda weighs around 16 tonnes or more, depending on how much water and fuel she's carrying at the time. Her air draft (height) above the waterline is roughly 4 metres (ca. 13 feet), and below the water line, she draws 1.2 metres (ca. 4 feet). Walking alongside as the tractor-trailer drags her from the yard to the launch slip, there's a lot of very-big-boat beside you.

The thought of everything that could break if something went wrong and she fell over is terrifying.

At the water's edge, a large travel lift with two U-shaped straps underneath is backed over the trailer and picked up the boat. With it now elevated even higher in the air, the travel lift moves it the short distance to the water, its wheels going either side of the slip. There, the boat is slowly lowered into the sea. All that weight and height rest on two 10 cm (ca. 4 inch) wide woven straps that will swing slightly if you give the boat a push.

We've hoisted and launched *Matilda* several times now, and it's always a nerve-wracking experience. While the yard crew are calm and collected, they launch or retrieve ten or more boats a day like this during the season; you also know that it's still a risky process. The supervisor films the whole process, not to post it on Instagram, but to keep a record and prove that they did everything correctly if something were to go wrong.

The captain we'd hired to help us move the boat, Nikos, was with us. He says, "Don't worry, they only drop one a day; it's okay"

Somedays, the Greek sense of humour is very Australian and dry.

As soon as *Matilda* touches the water, the yard crew lower the straps and drags them out from under the boat, and that's it. You're launched, and you need to quickly clear the slip for the next boat.

Nikos seemed non-plussed by it all. When *Matilda* hits the water, he jumps on board and disappears inside.

"The previous owner said that when we launched, we need to make sure we let water into the dripless seals[4] to lubricate the shaft..." I called to him.

"Yes, yes, no worries."

"No worries" wasn't going to cut it for me. I climbed aboard after him, opened the hatch to the seals, and pulled them back anyway, just like the previous owner had shown me on dry land. As the sleeve retracts, water starts gushing into the boat. Was that right? It's what I was instructed to do, but is water supposed to rush inside the boat like this? Fortunately, it stopped again as soon as I released them. I'm still unsure if I could have sunk the boat then and there before we'd even left the slip.

"Are the sea cocks opened?" Asks Nikos.

"Should be; I was told we were all ready to go."[5]

Thirty seconds later, the motors were started, the yard crew freed the lines, and Nikos guided us out of the slip. We were underway.

For two glorious minutes, you couldn't wipe the smiles from our faces as we headed out across Kilada Bay, finally free and afloat. We'd done it, all that hard work and effort leading to this moment. We were now aboard our own boat, and the dream had begun.

Then, an engine alarm went off.

"I can't read French", Nikos shrugged.

With the previous owners being French, the engine settings were in French. Which meant the errors were in French, too. And not just any French, but abbreviated French, enough so that Google Translate didn't understand what the error was trying to say.

While Nikos stopped the boat in the middle of the bay, Karina and I wrote down the error and dug through the manuals to no avail. All the manuals on the boat were in English, which ironically meant we didn't have a French version to try to match the error to.

---

4. Where the shaft that turns the propellor enters the boat, there's a seal which prevents water entering. For obvious reasons this is "dripless" as constant water entering a boat is generally considered a bad idea.

5. If you're experienced with boats, this blasé statement will horrify you as much as it now does me. Fortunately, we were in fact ready to go.

We searched online and found a French version of the manuals. Our best guess at attempting to translate the abbreviated message is that the alarm was warning us the coolant was a bit low.

"It's okay," says Nikos, "I just run this engine a bit slower."

We limped out of Kilada, our earlier enthusiasm replaced with the realities of what had just happened. We couldn't even make it two minutes from launch, let alone the ten nautical miles down the coast to the marina, without a problem.

Five minutes later, Nikos reports that the engine temperatures are reading the same for both engines, so if it is the coolant level, it's not a concern yet. He powers up, and we motor on south to Porto Cheli.

As nothing further goes wrong, the grins slowly creep back onto our faces, Nikos tells me to take the wheel, and finally, it all feels real. I'm sitting at the helm, sailing on the Greek seas, roughly twelve months after we hatched our original plan. It's happening!

Ten minutes later, we exit the bay, and the swell pushing down the Argolic Gulf hits us on the beam. The boat starts rolling wildly until Nikos takes over the wheel and points us across the waves.

"It's okay", I tell Karina, who's sitting gingerly in the rear cockpit, "we'll be around the corner soon, and it will feel better."

It's clear that she's having some second thoughts, but she's also toughing it out. We both knew there would be a few challenges. Still, it would have been nice to avoid having them all on day one. Then we're clear from the swell, and within an hour, we arrive at Porto Cheli and the marina.

When we'd hired a captain to assist us, we had a false impression of how involved they'd be. From Nikos' perspective, he knew how to turn the motors on and steer the boat; frankly, the rest was up to me.

With more experience and hindsight, I now have more sympathy for him. While the fundamentals remain similar, every boat is an assortment of different systems that have evolved since it was commissioned. It's impossible to move from one boat to another and "know" how everything works.

Perhaps elsewhere in the world, a different captain would take the time to understand all the systems before setting off. But Nikos was just a local fisherman, asked to move a boat a short distance in waters he'd sailed his whole life. Knowing how to turn the engines on and steer is almost all the skill he needed. Right until we tried to do something more complex.

As we pulled into the marina, the harbour master spoke to us on the radio and allocated us a berth where we needed to back in stern-to or "med moor". This somewhat complicated manoeuvre, common in the Mediterranean, involves dropping the anchor out in front of the boat, perpendicular to the dock, then reversing back to tie off.

"You have thrusters? You turn them on, please," Nikos instructed.

The wind was blowing strongly, and the thrusters would be essential to help position the boat.

I've never counted them all, but it's no exaggeration to say there are easily 40+ switches, dials, and systems on *Matilda* controlling things. I knew the thrusters worked, as I'd had a play with the joystick during the sea trial, but I'd never turned them on myself before.

The thruster control has two buttons labelled 'on'. I looked at it and decided it was straightforward enough. Two buttons. One for the bow thruster, one for the stern thruster. It's just a matter of knowing which.

I pushed one button, but nothing happened. I pushed the other, but nothing happened. I remembered being shown a battery cut-out switch for the rear thruster, so I went and turned that on. No joy. The thrusters are still not operational. Working through the options in my mind, I've clearly forgotten something important.

Under the helm is the master control panel. It's full of switches that control the systems on the boat. Looking over them, I couldn't see anything obviously labelled thrusters, although it's a possibility as everything was still labelled in French, too.

"Screw it," I thought as I flicked on all the switches I could see.

Still no joy, but a grinding sound started from the bowels of the boat.

It's at that point I smelt it—the stench of sewerage. One of the switches I flicked was the macerator, which pumps out the black water (sewerage tank).

At this point, the harbour master, who had been waiting to take our lines on the pier, visibly gave up. As he watched us venting sewerage in his harbour, unable to line the boat up with the thrusters while the wind continued to pick up, he directed us to give in and tie alongside instead.

Matilda had just arrived at her first port of call.

***

Four months later, we returned to Porto Cheli, and as I docked alongside myself, thrusters working but barely used, the same harbour master, Elias, was there.

"*Matilda*, welcome back. You're getting good at this," he called.

"Yeah, that first time was a disaster. Sorry about that," I replied.

"Don't worry about it. Everyone has a first time. You're doing good, you got better, that's what matters." He laughed as he walked off and called back, "Not everyone gets better!"

***

There are a few rare days in your lives where you'll learn more in 24 hours than at any other time in your life. Perhaps it's your first driving lesson. It could be the first time on campus at a University or a new job. Maybe it's that first day at home with a newborn baby.

In the middle of it all, it's overwhelming. Everything is confusing, but there's no option but to get through it. Logically, you know that in a week or two, you'll look back and think — why was that even an issue? But at that moment, you know it will continue to be overwhelming, and you have to be okay with that.

That first day of boat ownership is right up there with all those other life events. It's more than just the buttons (and there's SO MANY BUTTONS). A button is simple. There can be many of them, but when it's pressed, it stays pressed and (hopefully) something happens.

Take windshield wipers, press them on, press them off. Or the light above the helm station. Press the button, and the light turns on. Press it again, and the light turns off. While there are countless buttons, usually, they are easy to comprehend. The problem is the systems.

A boat, at its most basic, consists of a hull and a method of propulsion. A rowboat, for example, is nothing more than a shell to keep the water out, a seat, and a set of oars. As you increase in length and utility, you add more complexity.

The simple act of taking a shower aboard *Matilda* is non-trivial and entirely different from on land. It looks something like this:

1. Make sure the freshwater pump is on.

2. Ensure the shower sump pump is turned on, or the water won't drain.

3. Want hot water? Ensure you run the engines or the generator for an hour before showering.

4. Is there enough water in the tanks for that shower you want to take?

5. Do you have the right products? It should be ocean-friendly, as the shower sump drains straight into the sea.

6. And then something breaks. The bilge pumps are going off, everything stinks, and you have no idea why.

More than a button, it's a system. It's a complex series of interactions and failure points that are all key to a good experience.

Over time, it all becomes second nature, and you don't think about it, but when you're new to it all, you're left wondering why the shower is cold, filling with water and refusing to drain. It's not a remotely straightforward process at all.

The fact that we were initially not allowed to pilot *Matilda* ourselves was a blessing in disguise. We hired a second captain to relocate us the 60 nautical miles from Porto Cheli to Lavrion Olympic Marina so that we could be close to Athens and our powerboat course.

Instead of exploring the Mediterranean, we were trapped at the docks a few kilometres away from the nearest town, with all the time in the world to learn how to operate our new life living aboard.

Some systems were straightforward. The thrusters that wouldn't turn on? You press the two buttons labelled 'on' together, a safety feature to prevent accidentally engaging the thrusters. The French language setting on the engine controls? Our local Volvo mechanic switched it to English for us in under a minute and refused to charge.

Some were incredibly complex. Not necessarily because it was a problem when everything went right, but because when something goes wrong, complex systems quickly evolve into a long list of jobs to be completed.

Those first few weeks were a harsh introduction to the reality of boat life and how boat jobs breed. Most days, you cross one job off the list only to add two more. I don't believe there's a day we've owned *Matilda* that the list has ever reached zero. There's always something to repair, maintain or improve on a boat.

Eventually, though, during those first few weeks, we became more and more comfortable aboard. The systems began to make sense, and the jobs list, while not completed, was coming under control.

We understood enough to take small, controlled steps safely and with our powerboat training completed, we were ready to start travelling the seas. We set off on a shakedown cruise.

Seven

Footloose

"The boat is safer anchored at the port, but that is not the aim of boats"
— Paulo Coelho

T he first time I skippered *Matilda* was terrifying. Now the moment had arrived, the dream of setting off, footloose and fancy-free, to explore the world felt more like a nightmare.

All the training, all the practising on other boats, all the dreaming, and all the work to get our insurance and certificates in place. It felt too little. Right there at that moment, with over 16 tonnes of boat at my fingertips on the throttle, there were so many ways things could go wrong. More worryingly, if they went wrong, there was no one else left to blame but myself.

I'm not one to try difficult things on my own. Misery loves company. Karina, of course, was there. I knew that despite my internal doubts, she, at least, believed I could do it.

Our friend Camille was also on board. She'd heard us talk of almost buying a boat for several months and was excited to be there on the first voyage, blissfully unaware of how little we really knew. She also had some sailing experience of her own, a valuable addition to our small crew.

As our final guest, we had Yannis, the brother of our translator Ioanna. We'd tried to find someone with some power boating experience to join us, and Yannis, who also had his powerboat license, agreed to come for the ride.

I've taught many people how to pilot *Matilda* since, and I always point out the same thing: it's not the going that's hard. It's the stopping. And the not hitting things. It takes five minutes to learn how to start the boat, get underway from anchor and pilot around the coast in good weather. But it's never when things are going well that you need the skill.

At our marina in Lavrion, we were in a slip pointing out into the middle of the fairway. Visualise several long piers, all parallel to each other. Along each side of the pier are slips with small "finger docks" in between — like a car parking space, where the finger dock is the line between you and the boat next door. The fairway is the water that runs between the slips on the two piers.

In most cases, especially in Greece, you'll be docked stern-to in the slip, and if you look across the fairway, there is the bow of another boat roughly a boat length and a half across the water from you.

Having briefed everyone on their roles, started the engines, and tested the controls as many times as I could get away with, the moment of truth had finally arrived. We were going to slip the lines and move the boat for the first time with me at the helm and in command.

"OK, release the lines!" I called.

Yannis and Camille quickly released the lines, and I eased *Matilda* into gear. She quickly started to move forward out of the slip and into the fairway.

"You're getting close to the finger dock!" yelled someone from the stern.

I looked down at the wheel. Whoops, better centre the rudder. Okay, I should be going straight. Nothing happening? No worries, I'll use the thruster.

I tapped the bow thruster, and the bow gently pivoted away from the finger dock. Of course, it's a boat; unlike a car, it pivots around a centre of mass, so if the bow goes one way, then the stern goes the other.

"A fender is getting squashed!"

I confidently replied, "That's what the fender is for!"

We quickly picked up speed. As the water started to move over the rudder, I could finally begin to steer, but it was about now, halfway out of the slip, that I realised we were going too fast.

All boats have their quirks. *Matilda* is a trawler, meaning she's heavy and slow by design. The problem is, in a confined space, she's not slow enough. She has big, heavy propellors which move a lot of water and give her a lot of torque. If you idle in gear forward, she'll quickly start to do around three knots (a brisk, fast walking pace).

The adage is that when docking (or moving around docks), never go faster than you want to hit something. With 16 tonnes of momentum, 3 knots is too fast.

I was prepared for this. Like other boats I've been on, you can't really go slow on the throttle. Instead, you slip the boat back into neutral and let it continue forward until you lose momentum, then pop it into gear again for a few seconds. Rinse and repeat.

This dancing on the throttles quickly becomes second nature. If you watch a skilled captain, you'll see them flicking the throttles in and out of gear as they manoeuvre the boat. On a boat like *Matilda*, with twin engines, you can throttle the engines independently, putting one in gear forward and the other in reverse. A skilled captain can use the propellors opposing each other like this to quickly spin the boat around on its length or assist a tight turn.

I was not yet a skilled captain.

We had moved halfway out of the slip. I had the speed under control, but it felt like we were still rapidly closing on the boat across the fairway. With the finger dock on one side of our stern and a boat on the other in our berth, there was no room to actually pivot yet without hitting anything.

Finally, once we're three-quarters of the way out, I could start turning. Of course, now we had slowed so much that I lost steerage again. *Matilda* won't turn well using the rudders at such low speeds. The wind was also causing us to drift a little.

Boats tend to keep the momentum that they have. A car doesn't drift sideways, especially not at low speed, but boats do. Now that *Matilda* is mostly out of the slip, I've managed to turn her bow and point in the right direction. But, she's also still continuing to travel sideways, across the fairway and still moving towards the boat across from our slip.

A bit of reverse to slow us, some thruster to stop the sideways movement, then more thruster to correct the pivot that induced, and finally, we are free to move forward! Nowadays, I'd be much more comfortable coming close to the boat across the slip and then spinning in place, mainly with the engines and just a touch of thruster. Still, mission accomplished — we were out of the slip without hitting anything.

As we moved up the fairway, the wind blew on the bow, and we started fishtailing as I oversteered. This is partially because we were still going too slow to get proper steerage and partially because I had no idea where the centre was on the wheel and kept over-correcting. It would take another trip or two before I noticed the rudder indicator on the autopilot that displays the precise direction of the rudder.

Finally, we reached the end of the fairway and faced the challenge of navigating a 90-degree turn again, this time to head towards the marina exit.

I wish I could look back now and say that was one of the most stressful moments on *Matilda*, but in reality, it was nothing. It was a very anxious moment, but overall, it was a success.

We've been in a few situations since where if all that happened to us was coming out of a slip a little too fast and almost-but-not-really bumping a boat 5 metres away... Well, comparatively, that would be a cause for celebration.

We'd made it out, we didn't hit anything, and we were underway. Any docking (or departure) where you achieved the goal, no one got hurt, and no equipment was damaged is a success. Karina and I had just made those first critical steps on the ladder to more experience.

***

Remember, if the going is easy, it's the stopping that's hard.

For our first overnight, we travelled to Kithnos and the famous Kolonos Beach, a small spit of sand that splits two bays and connects with a small island, making it a peninsula.

I'm not suicidal. While I was inexperienced, safely navigating *Matilda* twenty nautical miles across calm seas was, if a little ambitious, still well within my abilities. The same goes for docking. While it was a challenge and not something I was eagerly awaiting to do on return, it wasn't outside my abilities, provided I took it slow and had good weather; we'd made a lot of effort to pick good weather windows. You have to start building experience somewhere.

What I was absolutely not that familiar with was anchoring. Like many first-time boaters in the Mediterranean, my experience of actually dropping an anchor was limited. Chartering and sailing in the San Francisco Bay, where I'd gained most of my experience, was always from dock to dock or dock to mooring ball. I'd also completed a charter in Greece with an experienced captain, where I met Camille. We'd both helped anchor on that trip several times, including tying to shore.

I'd read the books, completed a docking course and assisted with it various times. Even if I hadn't done it myself yet, I was at least comfortable with the theory and willing to give it a go. There was no time like the present to put theory into practice. The weather was good, limited boats were around (or so we thought), and we were all ready to learn something new.

Arriving at Kolonos Bay was an intimidating experience. Even with the tail end of Covid-19 still suppressing travel, there were enough boats out and about to make it a challenge. We cruised slowly through the bay, uncertain about what depth we should anchor at and nervous at the sheer volume of boats. Plenty of boats lined the side of the bay, moored stern-to to the rocks and eventually, I decided that was the best option for us. We'd do that too. Why not take the five minutes of practice I'd had at Med Mooring in San Francisco[1] three years before and now do it for real? All in the middle of a busy bay with boats tied seemingly at random everywhere to rocks.

Cue fifteen minutes of absolute chaos.

After dropping our anchor and reversing to shore, *Matilda's* bow kept drifting sideways. Camille and Yannis jumped into the water to swim the lines to shore. The lines kept sinking, at real risk of tangling the propellors — a danger I did not fully appreciate at the time.

We had no method of communication. Instead, I tried to yell at Camille in the water and Yannis on the rocks from the flybridge of the boat. Our lines weren't long enough, which meant we had to pull close to the shore — another thing that I thought little of at the time, but now I realise we were much closer than I'd accept today. After much yelling, gesturing and confusion, we got the stern tied down, but the bow continued to drift.

Panic and stress do strange things to your brain. What's completely obvious if you stop and think turns out to be incredibly difficult to understand while the adrenaline is running high. If you've ever done any form of emergency training, be it first aid, a PADI Rescue Diver course, lifeguarding or similar, you'll learn some form of the mantra "Stop, Breathe, Think, Act".

When things go wrong, we tend to want to throw ourselves into action immediately. Unfortunately, this often makes things worse. Even spending a few seconds to stop, take a breath, think through what some actions are and then act can make a big difference to your safety and the outcome of the action. Without this, you can quickly fall into a pattern of behaviour that solves the immediate issue but doesn't fix the root cause.

I had become more concerned with tying off the stern and the crew in the water swimming to shore, so I kept using the thrusters to bring the bow back to alignment. I never stopped to think about why the bow wasn't staying pointed towards the anchor.

---

1. Which was no more than dropping anchor and reversing the stern towards a dock without actually tying off.

Then, suddenly, the bow thrusters stopped working.

I've never quite figured out why they stopped. They worked fine the next day. The most likely cause was we'd either completely drained the thruster battery by overworking them for 10–15 minutes, or perhaps a protection circuit had tripped to prevent overheating. Whatever the cause, the one tool we'd been relying on was suddenly taken away.

With the thrusters off, the bow of *Matilda* slowly continued its inevitable drift towards the boat next door. Its bemused captain, who'd been watching us all this time, called out, "Captain! Would you like some advice?"

"Yes please!" I cried. I doubt he'd ever heard such a grateful exclamation in his life.

"Your anchor, it's not set. This is why your bow is drifting. You have to lift your anchor, go out, drop it again, put out much more chain, then reverse on it. Make sure your boat doesn't move, then let more chain out to come back and tie off. There is lots of weed here; it's hard to set properly."

We'd made the same mistake I've since seen novice captains make again and again. As we dropped the chain, we immediately started reversing in. Given there was close to 15 metres of water under the boat when we dropped anchor, there was no way it would have hit the bottom; we'd dragged it back a long way with us. By the time we stopped and pulled in the loose chain, the anchor chain was too short for the anchor to hold the boat properly.

If you're in fifteen metres of water, you need to drop at least fifteen metres of chain before you begin to reverse.

With the advice taken into consideration, we lifted the anchor, dropped it again, made sure it was set, and then tied off stern-to on our second attempt. The captain next door smiled and waved goodbye as I called out my thanks.

While we learnt a lot about anchoring stern-to and anchoring in general that day, surprisingly, it wasn't the most useful lesson. I'll return to anchoring shortly, but the lesson I've used the most since then is the simple technique of, "Captain, would you like some advice?"

It's a non-threatening way to approach someone to see if they'd like assistance. If the person says no, you walk away and leave them to it, but the majority of times, you'll get a very eager, positive response.

Moreover, ensuring the advice is somewhat "impersonal" can help. Of course, it was the weed that caused issues with our anchor! Not my complete and utter incompetence.

While I didn't believe it for a minute, I still appreciate the kind words and how they allowed me to save some face. The boating community is typically relatively kind to each other; we've all been there a first time, and occasionally, that first time has left a deep scar.

***

The importance of that shakedown cruise can't be overestimated. A short 3-day trip that forces you to use the systems while you're not too far from home base is invaluable. While there were a few niggles, the biggest issue was a blown anchor fuse which forced us to retrieve the anchor manually, a gut-busting effort hauling heavy chain and a lead-weighted anchor from the bottom.

Replacing the fuse happened back on the dock and required removing the guest cabin mattress and diving head-first under the bed into the bow of the boat. It quickly went on the list of needed modifications to improve safety and continue to further make *Matilda* ours.

After reflecting on the challenges of tying stern-to and realising the danger if the rope were to become trapped in the propellor, we decided to add floating lines: bright yellow lines, long enough to reach the shore and floating so they wouldn't sink and get tangled[2].

It was also clear that the starboard engine needed to be nursed through the season. Both the surveyor and the engine mechanic advised it would be fine, but the coolant system required an overhaul. Meanwhile, we had to keep topping up the oil and coolant levels until we were ready to haul *Matilda* back out of the water and address it properly.

We took another day trip with friends, a good excuse to practise leaving and returning to the dock, as well as anchoring in a bay for a day of swimming. Already on this second journey, we were much more in control, and things went smoothly.

While the list is never done, we slowly crossed off items that we fixed. A leaking hatch was replaced, the canvas was patched, a faulty gauge was repaired, and storage lockers were

---

2. Or so we thought. As you'll read later I significantly underestimated my ability to screw things up in an emergency.

rearranged to our liking. As we slowly gained experience in the basics of piloting *Matilda*, and the major repair items dealt with, it seemed we were ready to go.

Or were we? We could upgrade and address more things, but some would take weeks to resolve (and as we were quickly learning, boat weeks rapidly turned into boat months). Maybe there was no perfect? Maybe, just maybe, we weren't going to complete everything and needed to start our journey in a less-than-perfect state.

At its core, living on a boat is an adventure. That's not to say it's extreme in the same way as, say, climbing Mt Everest or cave diving, but it is inherently riskier than living on land.

At some point, you realise it's impossible to eliminate every risk or instantly repair everything. Instead, you manage it. You check the weather forecast, maintain your systems, and ensure that you have sensible backups in place, and as you gain more experience, you learn what's mission-critical and what you can safely put off.

Eventually, every boat worthy of the name has to put out to sea. Instead of staying safely tucked up into our dock, we were going to cast off the lines and go for real. With the year slowly ticking away, it was time to really liveaboard and cruise full-time without the comfort of a permanent home to return to.

We spent a lot of time deciding where to spend our first night. After considering all the options, we settled on Varkiza, a small beach suburb on the outskirts of Athens.

Two critical facts helped me make the choice. The first was simple. We were familiar with the area. We knew what we'd find ashore, and we had frequently seen plenty of boats anchored there.

The second consideration was the wind. The bay was sheltered from the prevailing north winds and should give us a calm and peaceful first night. With everything in place and a destination planned, we headed out of the marina for the final time, ready to anchor out for the first night of our new life.

***

We need to talk about anchoring for a moment. It's a big part of liveaboard boat life in the Mediterranean, and many of these stories revolve around the failure to do it properly. It's worth pausing here to understand how it works.

Conceptually, anchoring is simple. You toss a big piece of metal[3] over the front of the boat that's secured to the bow by rope or chain. For centuries, this was sufficient. The bigger and heavier, the better. It was essentially the weight of that big piece of metal that held the boat in place.

Today, anchoring technology has advanced considerably. Modern anchors, while still being a heavy piece of metal, do two critically important things.

The first is that they are designed to bite into the seabed. They achieve this in various ways, including carefully designed geometry, roll bars and lead weighting. A quality modern anchor, properly deployed, can generate far more holding power than its weight as it buries itself deep[4].

The second and somewhat contradictory thing an anchor needs to do is to let go. There's no point in an anchor that holds the boat so well that you can never move again! Modern anchors are designed so that as the chain is pulled vertically, the shank of the anchor levers upwards. This breaks the hold the anchor has with the ground and frees it.

Obviously, it would be bad if this lifting of the anchor happened unintentionally, as was the case when we first anchored at Kolonos Beach. To prevent this, the next important concept when anchoring is the length of the rode. The rode is the length of chain or rope (or occasionally both) that connects the boat to the anchor. In *Matilda's* case, and on most cruising yachts in the Mediterranean, the rode is all chain.

To prevent unintentionally lifting the anchor, you have to deploy enough rode that it can lie along the bottom of the seabed. As you'll remember, in Greece, the correct amount of rode in 5 metres of water is... 25 metres. I didn't even need to break your toe. This amount of chain ensures that as the boat is pushed by the action of current, waves, and wind, the rode is stretched out and pulls the anchor roughly parallel (and therefore biting deeper in) to the seabed, not up. It also helps prevent the anchor being pulled sideways as the boat swings in the wind.

The next critical consideration is what the bottom of the seabed is like. In general, rock is no good[5] – the anchor can't bite in to generate hold and, in the worst case, might get stuck under a boulder. Thick mud is okay; nice, deep, clean sand is the best.

---

3. a.k.a. the anchor

4. A well set anchor can barely be seen as it literally digs itself in under the seabed.

5. I say in general because it is possible to have an anchor specifically designed for rocky bottoms.

With these basics in mind, the next consideration is how the boat will swing around the anchor as the wind changes. Given the right seabed, the correct amount of rode and a well-set anchor, you'll stay securely fastened. But, as the wind swings around, the boat will spin in a circle around the anchor. You need to ensure you've left enough room for the boat so that you won't hit the shore, another vessel or other hazards when the boat lies in a different direction.

Finally, you want to ensure that there's not too much wind. Ideally, your chosen location is sheltered from the prevailing wind direction. You'll also check the forecast to understand what the conditions will likely be — the more wind, then the more room you need to swing, and the more rode you should put out to ensure the boat holds properly.

Congratulations! You've just learnt the basics of what every boating course and manual I've read teaches you about anchoring. To anchor the boat, find a sheltered bay with a nice bottom, preferably not too deep, with plenty of room for the boat to swing. You drop the anchor and deploy sufficient rode so that when the boat moves with the wind, the anchor bites, not releases.

***

With all this anchoring knowledge in mind and our hard-earned experience at Kolonos Beach, Varkiza seemed to be a perfect first anchorage. A short distance from the marina, it was a big, shallow bay with a sandy seabed. The wind forecast showed very light conditions on the night we decided to head there. Perfect for our first overnight alone.

We've anchored out hundreds of times since then, and that first night ranks as one of the worst we've ever had. The boat was rolling so hard that we both felt seasick. Cupboards were flying open, the sliding door to the main cabin was slamming back and forth until we worked out how to fasten it, and Rosie (our dog) vomited on our bed. We were miserable.

What the various courses and our experience to date had neglected to focus on was the effect of swell, the waves constantly rolling in from offshore. It's not inherently dangerous and (within reason) doesn't impact the safety of your anchoring. But, when the boat is rolling around, and you're constantly on the verge of throwing up, it does impact your enjoyment and quality of sleep.

As we've repeatedly discovered, while theory is critical, there's a massive gap between being theoretically safe and in-reality-comfortable. If the theory keeps you safe, experience teaches you how to enjoy yourself and have fun.

Swell is problematic because it often has little to do with the immediate local conditions. Big waves can be generated by storms a long way from your location and travel for days or weeks across a large enough ocean like the Pacific. Eventually, they arrive at your perfectly selected anchorage and turn a peaceful bay into a rollercoaster.

Passing ships and ferries also generate a lot of swell; without realising it, we'd selected an anchorage only a few nautical miles from the busiest commercial shipping route in Greece. Combine the wake from incessant shipping traffic with the swell rolling in from storms near Crete a few days earlier, and you have the recipe for a terrible night.

The following day, we rolled out of the bed we'd been clinging to, still safely anchored in the same location but desperate to get the hell out of there and move on.

From Varkiza, we crossed the Saronic Gulf and the shipping lanes, intending to stop on the western side of the isle of Aegina.

When we arrived, the hard-won experience of the night before showed us it was still far too exposed to the swell to be comfortable, so we pushed on. Two hours later, we arrived at the island of Poros and a much more sheltered inlet called Russian Bay.

We've learnt now that this has always proven to be the correct call. If you're not comfortable, then do something different. We now always have a plan A, B and even C for where we are planning to go.

The safest place to be is in a harbour, but safety won't reward you with the new experiences and stunning anchorages that make the trials of boat life worth living. Finally, we were truly footloose, exploring the seas. Our only way forward was to take our hard-earned experience and grow, to continue to develop as sailors and full-time liveaboards.

Eight

Broken

"Cruising is just fixing your boat in a series of exotic locations" —
Unknown (cruising sailors adage)

T he story of our life on a boat could be summarised as "and then something broke". At one point, it was a serious contender for the title of this book, but it seemed a little defeatist. It is, however, true.

Having arrived at our first truly safe harbour of Russian Bay, we luxuriated in the feeling of independence. Here we were, on our boat, provisioned, happy, safe and most importantly, still. The weather was warm, the water clear, and we were in no rush to go anywhere.

The island of Poros is just over an hour south of Athens on the fast ferries. It's got a permanent holiday vibe, mainly existing to service tourism, including the numerous Athenians that travel there for an easy escape from the capital. Russian Bay is so-called because of the supply base for Russian warships that were located there; the old warehouses that supplied the fleet still exist on its shores. Russia had an agreement with the Ottoman Empire to use the bay, and post the Greek war for independence, the Greeks honoured this for a time in recognition of Russia's support.

The charter season was in full swing, and we enjoyed relaxing, watching the boats come and go, stopping in "our" little bay for an hour or three before rushing off to their next destination. It's a magical feeling, having no deadline. While everyone else was hurrying to be somewhere, we had no specific goal beyond enjoying ourselves.

Eventually, though, there's only so much serenity you can handle at one time. The nearby main town of Poros beckoned. We began to crave its tavernas and beer, the chance of some social contact, and an opportunity to fill the water tanks. Russian Bay was great, but what else might we discover if we headed onward? We decided to head for the town quay for a night, then travel further the next day, past the island of Hydra and toward the Argolic Gulf.

While it's fair to say we had yet to master anchoring, we were much more confident about the process. We'd now stopped off several times without any problems, and most importantly, the boat had successfully remained where we'd placed it. What we clearly hadn't mastered was retrieving the anchor again. The previously blown anchor fuse was a foreshadowing of difficulties to come.

In theory, bringing up the anchor should be more straightforward than putting it down. Ideally, one person stands at the bow, watching the chain, and uses a series of simple hand signals to indicate to the person steering where to position the boat. The goal is to keep the bow of the boat directly above the chain so the windlass can haul it in with the least possible stress on both gear and crew.

Done properly, it's a well-choreographed dance, a freestyle tango where the person up in the bow leads and the helm follows. The boat dances gracefully around the twist of the chain, the windlass humming smoothly as the chain and the anchor are raised aboard. Occasionally, there will be a brief strain on the windlass when the anchor pulls out of the bottom where it's been firmly set and buried, and then you're off.

With an inexperienced crew, it's a little more like a drunken hippo stampeding around the anchorage. There are roars of frustration from the bow, unclear directions, and the boat lumbers to and fro, yanking on the chain as the helm overcorrects and overpowers the boat. Inevitably, panic sets in as the boat swings too close to a neighbour, then more panic when they overreact and swing back towards a boat behind them.

We were somewhere in between the two extremes. With our investment in training and our efforts in communicating, we managed to look like we'd done this before. Not quite the polished team we are today, but also somewhat coordinated and effective. Until we weren't.

As we hauled in the last 5 metres (ca. 16 ft) of chain, there was a loud crunch and a grinding of metal on metal as the windlass shuddered to a halt. The boat was free of the bottom, but the anchor was still stuck, hanging a few metres below the bow. The chain had leapt off the gypsy[1] and jammed. Bits of plastic from the chain guide had fractured and scattered across the deck, while the fuse, always problematic with any load, had blown once again.

Karina cruised us back and forth in the harbour while I first replaced the fuse (diving in upside down beneath the guest bed once more). With the windlass powered, I then tried to unjam the chain, but the damage was too severe and my experience too limited to be able to make a difference. While it wasn't yet an emergency, our tension levels were rising — with the chain jammed, we didn't have a readily functioning anchor. Having established that we couldn't resolve the windlass issue ourselves, the next obvious choice was to head into Poros and, instead of mooring stern-to, pull in alongside[2].

In Greece, most local ports are in the centre of the town and have a section of the quay set aside for tourist boats to drop anchor and moor. Almost exclusively during the peak season from May–September, these operate as stern-to.

We knew that our decision to tie alongside wouldn't be popular, but we didn't have much choice with our anchor out of commission. Approaching Poros, we saw a long pier running out from the quay and decided that, given the options, tying alongside here would be reasonably acceptable.

Predictably, shortly after we pulled in, the dock master came by and asked why we weren't stern-to. As soon as they understood the issue though, they immediately declared it wouldn't be a problem and pointed out the local mechanic who happened to be working on the boat next to us. It's been our consistent experience that while there are plenty of dos and don'ts when it comes to docking in Greece, people are always reasonable and willing to make allowances for a boat in trouble.

The mechanic quickly looked at the windlass, grunted, indicated he'd return and then disappeared. Tied securely to the quay, we sat back and relaxed with a cup of coffee. You just can't hurry things in Greece.

An hour or so later, he returned with a few tools, a lot of brute force, and unstuck the chain. We were able to stow the chain and then secure the anchor, but the windlass was no longer functional. Several plastic parts were broken, and a metal guide piece was bent out of shape.

---

1. The big toothed gear inside the windlass that moves the chain.

2. Sometimes referred to as "English mooring".

"No problem," he told us. "I need to take this metal piece back to the shop where I can straighten it out. I'll order the replacement plastic pieces; they should arrive by ferry soon." He promptly disappeared with the metal guide and enough pieces of plastic to identify the parts he needed to order.

In typical Greek fashion, he provided no contact details. We realised that not only was half our windlass now missing, but we also had no means of following up to ask when the work would be complete. Fortunately, we were becoming increasingly familiar with this very Greek style of work, so we settled in to wait. We trusted that, eventually, everything would come together. We just didn't know when.

Two days later, the mechanic arrived back at the boat. With the new parts in hand and the metal piece repaired, he quickly put the windlass back together, and we were once again free to move forward.

***

Another popular saying among sailors is that everything is broken on your boat; you just don't know it yet. While a windlass jamming, bits of plastic flying into the air, and the screech of metal against metal is dramatic, we've since learnt that it's not all bad when something breaks down in this way. At least you know exactly what's wrong!

The things that break with a bang cause a lot of stress and occasionally a short-term emergency, but it's the things that fail silently that we've found are generally the more significant, more expensive problems.

We never expected how vital sound is in the monitoring and maintenance of a boat. It's something you only appreciate with experience. If you do get a handover from the existing owner, it will cover physical things like "switch this to turn the lights on", not the more subtle but critical things like, "when the freshwater pump has that tone, the water's almost out".

Or, on *Matilda*, the very subtle difference in sound between the water pump and bilge [3] pump.

The absence of a particular sound might be a good thing, or it could indicate an issue. Take the bilge pumps. Obviously, if they continually activate, meaning that water is coming into the bottom of the boat, that's not great. Counter-intuitively though, if they

---

3. The bilge is the lowest part of the boat where water accumulates, usually when you least expect it.

never activate, is it that the bilge is dry, or is there something wrong with the float switch that triggers the pump?

In our case, it could also be the case that the new and inexperienced skipper accidentally turned the bilge pumps off.

The bilge pumps have three settings on the control panel – off, manual and automatic. When in automatic, they are triggered by a float switch, which activates as the water level rises, draining the bilge until the float settles back down and the pump turns off again. Manual forces them to operate constantly but will burn the pump out if there's no water. On a boat, you really want them set to automatic mode.

At some point in the preceding week, while familiarising myself with the bilge pumps again, I switched them to manual to test if they worked properly. Instead of setting them back to automatic, I'd left them in the off position. We motored on, blissfully unaware of the issue, happy that there were no unexpected noises.

Our starboard engine battery was continually showing low voltage, so we stopped off at Ermioni on our way around to the Argolic Gulf to get an electrical engineer to take a look.

When he came onboard, he quickly discovered that not only was the battery failing, but the battery compartment, which sits just forward of the rear bilge, was full of water. The battery was an easy fix; we decided to replace both the starboard and port engine batteries as they were mismatched, which suggested they'd been replaced separately before (generally not a good idea).

This fixed the engine battery warning problem, for the moment, and I drained the water without thinking too much further about it. I noticed I'd left the bilge pumps off, so I switched them to automatic mode again without worrying too much about how the water had made its way into the bilge to the degree it flooded out and over the batteries.

I say for the moment because eventually, the starboard battery failed again. It turns out the starboard alternator (that charges the battery) was faulty, so the starboard engine battery was being continually drained and poorly charged, shortening its life. The previously mismatched batteries indicated this had probably been an issue for a while. The failing alternator was something we'd discover later.

With the batteries replaced and the bilge once again dry, we headed off to continue to explore the Argolic Gulf. As we moved north into the Argolic Gulf, we found ourselves back in Kilada, this time on anchor, enjoying the bay and the local Neolithic caves. As we sat there, we noticed that the sound of the freshwater pump activating was increasing again. At first, we didn't think too much about it, but when it continued to happen every few hours or so, we concluded that there was probably a leak somewhere causing the pressure to drop, which activated the pump.

We spent a day testing taps and hunting leaks, all of which failed to resolve the issue. Then, while sitting there, a speed boat came past too fast; the wake caused us to start rocking, and the pump triggered. It was the moment of inspiration we needed! Digging deeper into the boat, we realised it hadn't been the freshwater pump we had heard but the bilge pumps. The bilges were full of water again.

And there you have it. Now that we were looking for the right thing, we quickly identified the problem. Water was running from under the bed in the main cabin, slowly filling the bilge. This was the cause of both the water covering the batteries and the reason that the bilge often activated with swell. The swell caused the water to slosh around, and the float would trigger.

The next challenge was to find exactly where the water was coming from. We pulled up the mattresses in the bedroom, which showed significant leaks on the seams of the stainless steel freshwater tanks stored under the bed. Once again, it was clear the previous owners had tried to make some repairs (with fibreglass), but it wasn't sufficient.

While it sounds dramatic (freshwater leaking inside the boat), in reality, it's not a critical issue. After all, you PUT the water on the boat in the first place; the problem is simply that it's not contained where it should be. Still, we wanted to resolve it, so we decided to pull up anchor and head back south to Porto Cheli again, where we could find some boat services and a mechanic.

As we lifted the chain to make our way there, what should happen but the windlass promptly jammed again. This time, I could free the chain myself, having seen how it was done previously, but it was clear the windlass was still causing issues.

Back to Porto Cheli, the closest marina where we could tie alongside, and we were greeted once again by Elias and his cheerful hello. The mechanic we contacted agreed the windlass was too worn and old and had reached the end of serviceable life.

So we splashed the cash to not only replace it but also rewire it and move the fuse to make it more accessible in the future. If you ever have a component that needs overload protection, especially if it is prone to overloading, make sure you can reach it and reset it. The expense of fitting a circuit breaker you can reach around and flip on again is much more effective than having to regularly replace fuses upside down and beneath a bed in emergencies.

Tied alongside at a dock also gave us the confidence needed to tackle the freshwater tank. We emptied it and pulled it out from under the bed to try patching it further, but while we slowed the leak, we couldn't stop it. Several calls to mechanics and boatyards quickly revealed we were out of options — they were all flat-out dealing with the boats of people who'd been absent during Covid-19 lockdowns. There was no way we could get the tanks replaced before the end of the season.

Matilda had a leak, and we were just going to have to put up with it. For the remainder of that first season, the bilge pumps would activate numerous times a day as the tanks slowly leaked freshwater into the bilges. At the top of the winter haul-out list were new water tanks, a process that involved having custom food-grade tanks made to the correct dimensions and then installed.

With the windlass now working reliably, we topped off the freshwater and off we went. We finally made it up past Kilada and headed north to Nafplio.

***

Knowing your bilges intimately[4] turns out to be another unexpected maintenance skill. It's part of my regular checks now, ensuring everything looks like it should. It's a task significantly helped by the fact that with a couple of seasons under my belt, I now know much more about what *Matilda* should look and, importantly, sound like.

While the tanks were freshly replaced over winter, it's still not the last of the issues we've had with water.

Another time, the tanks emptied unexpectedly quickly. Before heading out for a walk we'd checked the water levels and turned the washing machine on. We returned to the sound of the pump running dry, damaged because there was no water to pump through it. Thinking that perhaps the gauge was faulty, we filled the tanks again and decided to wait and see.

When the tanks again emptied much sooner than expected, we moved to physically inspect them to see what was happening. Fortunately, this time, it was a quick fix. A mechanic who worked on the rudder (behind the water tanks) had bumped a lever and turned off the connection that drained water from the top to the bottom water tank. We'd

---

4. Which I confess is a sentence I never thought I'd write.

been running on less than 50% of our water volume. Switching the tap to open again was the fastest I've ever fixed a boat problem.

Another time, we again noticed the bilges filling with water. After a week of trying to diagnose the issue, a process that involved checking the tanks and every hose and tap in the freshwater system for leaking water, we'd made no progress. Then, during a regular engine room check, I noticed salt buildup at the rear of the port engine. The most likely cause was salt water leaking in somewhere that was drying out and leaving a salt residue behind.

This time, I went down into the engine room with the engines running, something I've now added to my regular checklist, and saw a leak from the elbow of a stainless-steel pipe exiting at the rear of the port engine. While we were underway, water spurted from a rust spot in the elbow, slowly running down into the bilge. At the point where it landed on the engine, it was drying out and creating a build-up of salt.

While it was an easy fix to have the elbow replaced, which stopped the leak, a lot of damage was already done. Despite cleaning the salt buildup at the time, six months later, we had a lot of repair work to do at the end of the season. The propellor shaft had to be polished because of rust caused by the salt water. The port gearbox housing was removed, sandblasted, and powder coated again due to rust and the electric solenoid on the gearbox was replaced, on the verge of failing from corrosion.

Maintenance is never-ending, and one problem frequently leads to another. You can't avoid it; it's an unavoidable part of boat life. But, if you know what looks, feels, and sounds right on your boat, you can frequently identify issues before they become a pricier and potentially disastrous issue.

It's incredibly satisfying to undertake a task and know that you've immediately made a difference. The water pump is now replaced, the tank has stopped leaking, and you have the skills and confidence to fix a thing if it goes wrong again.

The reality of boat life often feels like a never-ending list of problems that need to be resolved, but despite this, it's immensely satisfying. In my previous working life, I felt that what I did mattered, but I rarely experienced the joy of instant feedback.

The lesson we needed to learn was that on a boat, everything is broken; you just don't know it yet. But there's also a joy that comes from overcoming adversity and making it work despite the issues. Gradually, we continued to grow in confidence, and problems became a challenge to overcome rather than a reason to race back to base.

***

We spent those first few months around the Saronic and Argolic Gulfs for several pragmatic reasons, perhaps most importantly because it was a safe cruising ground with which I was familiar. But there was another reason, too.

During Covid-19, the plastic required to print ID-type cards (like driver licenses, national IDs and captain licenses) was in short supply across Europe due to supply chain issues. At least, this is the excuse we were given when the port police who issued our licenses said we could only have a temporary paper one that lasted three months.

"Three months? What do I do after three months?" I asked the port police officer issuing the temporary license in Glyfada, where we had taken our exam.

"You come back, we give you a new temporary one for another three months," she shrugged barely apologetically.

While annoying, it seemed it wouldn't be a huge problem. It gave us more reasons to stay in proximity to Athens. There was more than enough to learn and experience without setting off to cross the far reaches of the Mediterranean. At the time, though, it felt like yet another wrench in our plans after so many other setbacks.

The three months passed quickly, and we returned to Glyfada to renew our almost expired paper licenses. The timing had worked out well. Camille's birthday party was that weekend, so we left *Matilda* in Ermioni. Dimitris, the local fisherman who helped us move her to Lavrion, agreed to watch her, and we caught the fast ferry back to Athens.

It was the perfect plan. A weekend away, a party, some shopping in the big city, and pick up our new licenses while we were there. On Friday morning, we headed out to the port police, ready to renew our license.

"No. I can't renew this!" Said the port police officer at the counter forcefully.

"What do you mean that you can't renew it?" I was incredulous; we'd come a significant way primarily for these new licenses and had tickets booked on the ferry to return to *Matilda* again on Monday.

"It's not expired yet!" she stated as if this were utterly self-obvious.

"Well, of course it's not expired yet. It expires in three days on Monday, but we won't be here then," I tried to explain.

"Well, you must come back on Monday. I cannot replace it until it has expired."

No matter how many ways I tried to explain that we were leaving Athens on Monday morning and needed the license renewed to continue cruising, the officer just flat refused.

She was starting to dig her heels in. This was not going to end well. It turns out that what was broken now wasn't anything on the boat but instead the incomprehensible intricacies of Greek bureaucracy.

Suddenly, there was a blast of exasperated Greek over my shoulder. Another lady, who'd been listening to the proceedings, decided to weigh in on our behalf. She spoke better English than the officer on duty and fluent Greek. I cowered, caught in the crossfire between two angry women as voices and tempers raised.

Then, the officer behind the counter reached across and grabbed our existing licenses that she'd been refusing to take only moments before.

"Give me," she growled, then proceeded with the most forceful display of stamping I've ever seen. She seemed to be trying to drive the stamp through the paper and into the desk.

As she headed towards the back of the room to get the Captain to sign the new licenses, the lady who'd intervened on our behalf smiled sweetly and said, "Sometimes, these people just need to be told to do their jobs."

New licenses in hand and bureaucracy thwarted — this time — we were good to continue cruising. Two days later, our permanent licences arrived, and we had to head back to Athens and Glyfada again to collect them.

Nine

Friendship

"Any damn fool can navigate the world sober. It takes a really good sailor to do it drunk." — Sir Francis Chichester

I'm not saying that you have to drink alcohol to be a full-time cruiser, but a tolerance for drinking and the ability to mix a mean cocktail are unexpectedly useful skills.

Cruising can be a solitary lifestyle. When you're crossing oceans for weeks at a time, the ability to keep yourself sane and occupied and not kill your fellow crew is crucial. Coastal cruising in the Mediterranean, however, skipping from anchorage to anchorage, is anything but isolated.

Just the simple act of pulling into an anchorage triggers a complex series of social interactions, sometimes more than you bargained for. Do you know the correct etiquette for greeting a fellow sailor while they are naked at the bow of their boat? While we're not especially prudish about nudity, we don't have the same laissez-faire attitude towards it that some European sailors do.

With our water tanks and windlass under control, we'd taken the opportunity to head south. We dropped anchor in Gerakas harbour, a small, sheltered bay just north of Monemvasia on the Peloponnese. As we were tidying away after our journey, a small tender with a middle-aged couple on board pulled out from the dock and headed to the one other sailboat already anchored in the harbour.

They smiled at us as they came by, and we had a brief chat before they carried on to their boat for the evening. They were Germans, they liked the harbour, and they'd just had a lovely meal ashore.

Within 2 minutes of arriving at their boat, they were both back up on deck, completely naked, with a beer in one hand and a cigarette in the other. We've certainly met our share of sailors who like to swim naked. Until today, we had not yet met the more hardcore variety of nudists—those who try to spend the majority of their time onboard without clothes.

We shrugged it off. It's their boat; they are in the cockpit; I guess they can do what they want. Then, a new boat pulls into the harbour. In a flash, the German man puts down his beer and walks up to the bow of his boat, still completely naked.

One hand on his hip, waving with the other, he cried out to the approaching boat, "Hallo! How are you? I have 30 metres of chain out. Welcome!"

To this day, I'm uncertain if he really was just friendly or if it was all part of a cunning plan. The boat that arrived anchored just that bit further away than they needed to. I'm still unsure of the correct etiquette for greeting fellow sailors while nude, but if I ever do want a bit more room at anchor, I know one more thing to try now.

***

In our first few weeks travelling, meeting fellow cruisers was a challenge. There's a set of social cliques on the water that are not always obvious to the novice sailor. As a general rule, these cliques don't mix; like all cliques, they have their own social rules you need to learn. Once you know them, it's easy to quickly find the people who will enjoy being social with you.

Take superyachts as an extreme example. In the waters around Greece, we've moored near some of the largest superyachts in the world on several occasions. Despite the number of times we try to invite them aboard *Matilda* for a drink, they won't join us. It's equally frustrating that they never ask us aboard their 50-100 metre (ca. 160-320 ft.) yacht either! When you're chartering a superyacht for many €100,000s a week, you really don't want to share the experience.

While it's obvious you're wasting your time trying to chat with superyacht guests (the crew are often very friendly, though), what surprised us in that first season was that charter boats are also reserved when interacting with others too. Once we understood more about them, it made sense.

Your typical charter boat costs between €3,000-€12,000 per week depending on model, size, berths, age and, of course, the time of the season. Usually, that cost will be shared by a group of friends or family. They are together, in the Mediterranean, for two weeks on the holiday of a lifetime. They tend to look inward to each other for their entertainment. We've found them willing enough to have a polite conversation, but the reality is that they are there to party together, hit the tavernas and hang out with their existing family and friends. Chatting with charterers is fine, but it's pointless if you want to build a more robust social connection and perhaps meet someone to share a drink and dinner with.

Then there's the liveaboard sailors. People who are living on their boat for an extended period, whether full-time or for months during the year. You won't hit it off with everyone, but most people in this group are almost always willing to drop everything, hop onboard and drink your alcohol at a moment's notice.

Once you understand the rules, you can find someone interesting to talk to in under five minutes and be sharing a drink within six.

Great! So, you want to meet fellow liveaboards, and you'd like to minimise the time you spend trying to chat to charterers or superyachts who aren't interested in socialising? How do you know who is who?

Superyachts are easy to identify. See that shiny yacht with a full-time crew? The one worth €4 million+ and is at least 25 metres (ca. 82 ft) long? It's probably flagged somewhere like the Cayman Islands or Monaco. See the jacuzzi on the back? Perhaps a helicopter is on the top deck if it's big enough? The yacht that you would desperately love to have a tour of and see how the rich and famous live. Yeah, that's a superyacht. Forget it. It's not going to happen.

The difference between a charter boat and a liveaboard can be much more subtle.

Occasionally, it's easy. A dead giveaway for a charter boat is the name of a charter company emblazoned on the sail bag or the boat's hull. It can be more challenging to pick them from a liveaboard without that.

A good indicator that someone is a liveaboard will be the flag they are flying on their boat. If you're cruising in Greece, most boats (and charter boats) will be Greek flagged, but liveaboard sailors cruise widely and typically have a non-Greek country as the boat's flag of registration. There's a hierarchy to the country flags on a boat; *Matilda*, for example, is typically flying three, each one telling you something different.

The most prominent — usually in the centre of the boat at the stern, is the flag for the country of registration. This tells you who has legal jurisdiction over the vessel. It's not always a good indicator of the nationality of the people on the boat, but it's a good start.

If the boat is flagged in Australia, then there are almost certainly Australians aboard. If it's flagged in Poland, then you probably won't know where the owner is from, but in Greece, it won't be a charter boat. *Matilda* is flagged in Poland, a European "flag of convenience" country that meets the legal requirements we need.

On the starboard side of the boat, you'll see a courtesy flag — a country flag indicating the boat is legally in the waters it's currently sailing in. In Greece, a UK-registered boat will have a Royal Ensign at the stern and then a Greek flag on the starboard side.

The third set of flags, usually on the port side, are personal and bargee flags. These might be flags of the sailing club you belong to or a flag that indicates something you've achieved under an official organisation (like crossing the Atlantic as part of the ARC – Atlantic Rally Crossing). Typically, in the Mediterranean, the personal flag will be a country flag indicating the nationality of the people on board. It's not uncommon to see more than one if there are people aboard from a few different countries.

If you're in Greek waters and see a Greek flag on the stern and a French flag to port, it's most likely to be a Greek-registered charter boat with French people on board.

In *Matilda's* case, you will see a Polish flag on the stern if we're cruising in Greece, a Greek flag to starboard and an Australian flag to port. This means we're a Polish-registered vessel, legally cruising in Greece with Australians on board. This type of set-up is almost always indicative of liveaboard sailors.

Or perhaps it's a French flag on the stern and a Greek flag on the starboard. It's a French-registered boat cruising in Greek waters with French people on board. There's no need to repeat the personal flag because the nationality of the boat and the cruisers matches.

The equipment is another key indicator of a charter boat vs. an owner-cruised boat. If it's fitted with Starlink internet services or a radar on the mast, it's not a charter boat. Charter boats are generally very basic in fit-out. This is usually one of the first things you'll spot at sea.

The final giveaway is inflatable toys! I've yet to meet a liveaboard that travels with a giant pink flamingo tied to their boat. In summer, it feels like 50% of the charter boats in Greece have one of these ridiculous large toys tied down to the foredeck.

***

Having found a likely liveaboard, you need to break the ice and say hello if they haven't already done so first. This was a challenge in the first few months of cruising because it involved unlearning some common social rules that don't apply to boats. If you parked your car at the supermarket and started chatting to everyone nearby that you don't know, most people would think you are a bit strange.

Fortunately, liveaboard sailors are almost always willing to say hello. Instead of being scared off by strangers, we all welcome the chance to get "outside the boat" and talk with someone new.

When you're at anchor, the simplest way to meet someone is to cruise past on the tender and say hi. Especially in summer, everyone is hanging around outside or swimming. If you're pretty confident it's a liveaboard, then the most straightforward opening lie... I mean line... in the world is "Love your boat!"

It doesn't matter how beat up, run-down or decrepit it is. There's no sailor in the world that won't lap that up and launch into a history of where their boat was built, its previous life and how they ended up with her[1].

At harbour, it's a little different. As the boats are stern-to, you can walk up and down the quay and say hi; it works, but it isn't always the most effective way. With endless landbound tourists also wandering the docks, you don't get a great hit rate — we're often a bit wary of landlubbers. The best way to meet someone new when you're in port is to help out and catch lines.

Generally, the town quays in Greece are unorganised, boats coming and going and dropping their anchor and reversing stern-to wherever there's a gap. While it's possible to tie off with your crew (by reversing close enough to have them step to shore and catch your lines), it's far easier with someone on the shore to catch the lines for you.

As we sit back in the evening, watching the show unfold in front of us, I'm always quick to jump up and run to catch the lines of a boat backing in. The process is revealing as to the sort of person that's on board in terms of experience and sociability.

The charter boats early in the week[2] are usually a mess. The stern lines are all set wrong, positioned over the lifelines; the boat is stuck too far from the quay because the

---

1. Traditionally (in English), ships and boats are referred to as 'she / her', because of the latin origins of the word which was feminine. A more modern usage is to simply say 'it'. I prefer the tradition.

2. Charters typically change over Saturday, so on Sunday and Monday most skippers are still learning their boat.

person on the anchor won't let out enough chain, and the skipper is stressed and yelling instructions. We try to guide them in, but getting someone who's inexperienced and stressed to understand they need to un-cleat the stern line and retie it from the outside of the lifelines is a challenge.

While a boatload of charterers will generally hang out together, if the skipper seems amenable and if warranted, I've always proffered a gentle "Captain, would you like some advice?" This typically leads to a friendly conversation about how things went and, if desired, a few tips on improving. Occasionally, we've even run impromptu rope-throwing courses with the crew on the shore to get them ready for next time.

When an experienced liveaboard sailor backs down, their attitude towards the person on shore is critical. Are they grateful and appreciative, or do they bark orders at us when we're clearly already doing the right thing? It's the skipper's boat, and I'll always ask, "Where do you want the line to go?" Do they want to cross lines and put them out wide, or just run it straight back from their stern?

But, when they scream at you to tie off on the leeward side first, yell at you to "throw it back, throw it back" while you're still threading it through the loop or carry on and be unpleasant... it's a fair bet we're not going to get on. We'll get the lines secured, shrug it off, and go back to watching the next boat come in.

Eventually, though, you'll meet the experienced liveaboard couple that's been here and done it all before. They appreciate the help you're offering, and they can tell by looking you know what you're about. If you don't, they'll gently coach you to make it right. The process is usually relatively calm, even when the wind isn't, and you'll crack a joke or two with them as they secure the boat. At this point, the next step is simple.

I'll break the ice with, "Welcome to Porto Cheli. Have you been here before?" We'll exchange a few pleasantries and maybe share some essential information like "The water truck comes by 9 am every morning" or "You can get a key for the power from the office over there."

Another mistake I often made in those first few weeks was to stay and chat for too long. It's the wrong thing to do. No matter how friendly you are, when you've just completed a crossing, regardless of how long or how rough it was, you need some time. You want to tidy away the boat, clean yourself up, debrief, take a breather and relax. Imagine hopping off a long international flight; the last thing you need is in-depth pleasantries with a stranger, no matter how friendly.

With the introductions out the way, I'll say, "Well, I'm over there on *Matilda*; we usually have cocktails at 5 pm — you're welcome to join us for a drink when you're ready. No rush."

It works more than you might think. Most liveaboard sailors love a chance to get on board and look at someone else's boat! And the sort of person that responds to that open invitation is almost always someone we're happy to meet.

It was confronting when we started chatting with more experienced sailors. We weren't sure that we'd have anything to contribute. We shouldn't have been concerned. The simple fact you visited a given anchorage the day before means you have information to share about the latest local conditions that a more experienced sailor heading in that direction will appreciate. And, of course, day by day, you're gaining experience too.

Some of the kindest, most generous and knowledgeable sailors we've met have also been the most humble. Teasing out information from novice boaters like ourselves without making us feel stupid. The best sailors strive to improve, and even those with a couple of circumnavigations under their belt understand better than anyone that local knowledge and experience are invaluable. There's always more to learn.

***

It was this simple invitation to cocktails that introduced us to Mark and Elizabeth. We first met them in Ermioni while we were replacing our batteries as they docked stern-to in some tricky wind conditions. They were an experienced sailing couple, skills a little rusty after a long break from sailing.

Once they were safely tied off, I left them to settle in with an invitation to swing by and visit us on *Matilda*. An hour later, we heard a knock on the rear of the boat, and there they were, keen to meet up and say hi.

Ultimately, cruising, even as a full-time liveaboard, is a passion and hobby. You'll find plenty in common to chat about with fellow enthusiasts, and then from there, the conversation and relationship grow. Mark and Elizabeth are unique among couples we've met in that they first met each other on a flotilla holiday in Greece years before.

We had a lot to talk about and learn from each other, sharing our knowledge of local ports and learning from them about some of their sailing experiences. A margarita or two later, and then it was farewell. Ships crossing in the night, and off we went.

What we never considered initially is that the cruising grounds are smaller than you'd expect, and everyone converges towards the same locations. A few nights later, a boat came to dock in Porto Cheli. I went to catch the lines and who should it be, but Mark and Elizabeth again.

This time, there was a lot more joking around; they'd refreshed their skills and regained their confidence. They were also happy to see a familiar face. A dinner together ashore, an invitation from us for them to use the very fancy showers at the marina, then dinner aboard *Matilda* the night after, we set off our separate ways again as firm friends.

Eight months later, I invited them to join me as crew on a boat delivery[3] I made around the Peloponnese. It's hard not to like a couple with the same sense of adventure. When I asked, "Can you be here in Greece next week to help deliver a boat?" they quickly tossed aside their work to fly out and join in the fun.

A few months later, they were back in Porto Cheli, landbound this time on holiday, as we came past in *Matilda* and stopped in to enjoy dinner with them. We'll likely see them again this summer as we head back that way.

Of course, it doesn't always happen like this. More often than not, brief, intense friendships flare and fade as you go your separate ways. We get good at dealing with a feeling of grief for the friendship that might have been. Despite this, it's worth it every time.

We stay in touch online with many of the people we met, even those we saw for only one or two nights and may never see again. The cruising community is full of kindred spirits, people you want to get to know.

***

Despite the transitory nature of these connections, we've also discovered that it's common for even the most mundane of interactions to lead to long-term friendships. Having finally made it north of Kilada, now with windlass, batteries and our leaking tank under control, we were in the small harbour of Vathy. It was a typical, picturesque fishing village, a closed bay, with tree-lined slopes and a series of tavernas at one end.

---

3. Moving a boat from point A to B for some practical purpose beyond cruising. Charter fleets have a lot of deliveries at the beginning and end of the season as they reposition their fleets to and from their winter base to the cruising grounds.

I was flying my drone to take footage when a sailboat entered the harbour under sail. Typically, when this happens (sailing into a harbour), either the person knows precisely what they're doing, or they have no clue. It was clear this person knew exactly how to handle their boat and it was magical to see.

With the drone already in the air, I snapped a few photos of them — everyone who lives on a boat loves footage of themselves underway, as it's generally hard to obtain. I made a few passes; then later, once they'd settled on to anchor, I headed over in *Tilly* the tender to say hi.

"Would you like some drone shots of your boat coming into the harbour?" I asked.

Markus, a serious-looking German man with a grizzled grey beard, sat in the cockpit of his boat *Tara* and asked, "What are you charging?" while holding a beer.

"Nothing; I was just flying the drone when you came in and thought you might like some photos".

"Ah well, in that case, come on board and join us! Would you like a beer?"

We exchanged email addresses, and after a pleasant hour or so aboard *Tara*, I headed back to *Matilda* and emailed the photos over. They departed the following day, and we thought that was it.

A few days later, we headed back into Porto Cheli to shelter from some strong winds, and as we dropped anchor in the bay, we saw a couple waving madly from a nearby boat shouting out.

"Hello, how are you!" they cried.

I turned to Karina and asked, "Any idea who they are?"

It's one of the challenges aboard *Matilda*. We're very recognisable. As one of the few trawler-style boats around our cruising grounds, we're distinctive to most people we meet, but to us, all sailboats tend to look the same!

Karina says, "I think it's that boat you took the drone photos of. They had a red stripe."

She has always had a better memory than me for these things. I checked back through the photos and, sure enough, a red-striped boat. It was *Tara*. We decided to invite them aboard, so I sent another email asking them to join us for margaritas. Not long after, they set off in their tender and came aboard.

Several cocktails later, we parted on good terms, upgrading from email to sharing phone numbers, which proved useful when I received a phone call the next morning.

"Hallo! Sorry to wake you. Can you help me fetch my tender?" asked Markus.

It was a timely lesson that simple mistakes can happen no matter how experienced you are. I might also be partially responsible, as the margaritas[4] we make onboard *Matilda* are strong. They've caught more than one innocent visitor unawares!

Having returned to *Tara* the night before, instead of pulling their tender up onto the deck, Markus had tied it off and gone to bed. With the winds and swell in the night, it had pulled free and drifted away. A quick trip to the windward shore in *Tilly*, and we secured both his tender and the friendship with the simple act of helping each other out after sharing a few drinks.

Markus and Isa turned out to be great companions. Isa is friendly, compassionate, caring and a delight to know. Markus is gruff on the surface, with a heart of gold. He's incredibly knowledgeable about sailing, having been sailing since he was young and cruising the world since his early 20s. He has no time for fools but is always generous when sharing his knowledge and experience with eager learners. Perhaps his most surprising trait is an unexpected soft spot for stray cats, often disappearing during dinner to buy food to put out for the local strays if he feels they are underfed.

One of the great relationships when cruising is "the buddy boat". People you travel with who know you, know your plans and are looking out for you. At one extreme, it's literally cruising together, a helpful relationship, especially when travelling in more remote regions. At the other end of the spectrum, it's more a general awareness of where each other is, a sharing of news and seeking opportunities to meet when you're in the neighbourhood.

We met Markus and Isa several times that season and, at the end of the year, decided to put our boats up together in the same yard on the north side of Aegina.

Wherever you go around Greece, you'll meet lots of like-minded people. There's a new friend to be made in every port or at each anchorage if the right opportunity presents itself.

The lament of an old sea salt we met recently was, "I sail to get away; where can you go anymore?" I think the answer is you can't. Sailing is inherently a social sport. We all cluster to the same anchorages for the same reasons: shelter, proximity to attractions and scenery.

---

4. And delicious! 25ml cointreau, 25ml good tequila, 12.5ml mezcal, 25ml fresh squeezed lime juice (strained). Agave syrup to taste. Shaken with 2 ice cubes. Pour and serve over 2 fresh ice cubes.

In the same breath, he was dismissing some more remote ports that we loved because of the uncertain bureaucracy, the less-than-stellar marinas and uncertain weather conditions. There are plenty of reasons most people don't go there. Even so, we met many fantastic fellow sailors in these less popular locations.

Unless you want to spend a lifetime cruising across the oceans, interactions with fellow cruisers are a big part of everyday life. It wasn't what we expected, but we're glad it is. You can't truly get away, at least not in the Mediterranean, and we're okay with that.

Ten

Harbour Cinema

"Only two sailors, in my experience, never ran aground. One never left port, and the other was an atrocious liar." — Don Bamford

One of the simple joys in any anchorage is the cocktail hour, sitting back with a drink, discussing the day and enjoying the latest episode of Harbour Cinema unfolding in front of you. It was Markus and Isa who introduced us to the term Harbour Cinema. We'd already been indulging but didn't have a good name for it. It's a fairly universal pastime.

Harbour Cinema simply means sitting back and watching the boats anchoring, docking and manoeuvring in front of you with varying degrees of success, ideally with your favourite drink in hand. Some days, there'll be a blockbuster new episode, a disaster that fuels conversations for weeks. On most days, you're at least guaranteed a re-run of popular shows.

We've yet to meet a cruiser who doesn't enjoy a good session. Of course, there's always pleasure in watching a skilled captain manoeuvre a 25-metre (ca. 82 ft) yacht with metres to spare, dropping their anchor just so and backing down perfectly. But the highlight is always watching and learning from the mistakes of other crew when things go wrong.

It sounds crueller than it is. In reality, the experienced skipper sitting back with a drink, providing a running commentary to their crew about the mistakes some skipper is making, will also be the first to run and help catch the lines, ensuring everything is fine.

During the height of the season, entertainment is unavoidable as large numbers of inexperienced captains try to navigate tight harbours for the first time. Most novice skippers and crew make the same mistakes repeatedly, which are simple in practice and quickly corrected without real issues. Embarrassing perhaps, but rarely dangerous.

A part of the pleasure is also somewhat self-congratulatory. An indulgence as you realise, "We don't make that mistake anymore". One of the universal reasons I think we all enjoy it is because we've all been there before.

***

Despite being relative novices still, by the time we'd met Markus and Isa, we had begun to gain plenty of hard-earned experience.

Experience is one of these things that's both easy in theory — you just need to get out there and spend time on the water — but difficult in practice. Most people cannot make the same decision as us and choose to live this lifestyle full-time, although I do believe that some of them could make this a reality if they decided to.

Still, the reality is, while we were able to say "fuck you" and run away to sea, most others have not. Regardless of where you start from, you quickly become experienced at something when you're doing it full-time. Once you liveaboard, you'll soon find that most people you meet on boats have less practical experience than you.

It's simple math. In our first season, we spent around twenty weeks cruising full-time on *Matilda*, anchoring in a new port almost daily.

You meet sailors, often charterers, who confidently say, "I've got twenty years of sailing experience." In reality, that typically represents a two-week holiday every other year for the last ten years and maybe a couple of day trips while they are home twice a year. Which works out to roughly the same twenty weeks of actual on-water experience we accumulated in our first season.

Because they are chartering, it's also usually a "fair weather" experience, too — charters run during the time of year with the best weather after all. As liveaboards, we're out there in fair weather and foul, from far too early in the season to its bitter, cold and blustery end. Storms and foul weather aren't pleasant, but your confidence and abilities increase once you survive a few.

Of course, we're still relatively inexperienced, too. We constantly meet liveaboards and the occasional charterer, who have been doing this for years. They've gone further, gone harder and even circumnavigated. For the most part, we've just been tootling around Greece.

But, even with plenty of experience, you'll regularly face challenges.

For most liveaboard cruisers, a vast amount of cruising is going somewhere you're unfamiliar with. Which means that, when we get there, we all fumble around a harbour trying to work out where to anchor or grind our keel when we end up somewhere shallower than indicated on the charts. All things destined to make us the next feature item on Harbour Cinema.

Even for highly experienced charterers, when they hop onto that boat for the first time in the season, they'll be dealing with the fact that everything is unfamiliar. They are still trying to get a feel for the way their boat handles, while still thinking of that argument they had with Bob-from-accounting. Wherever their mind is, it's not in the moment, as they try to moor stern-to for the first time in a year.

I said earlier that it's the "not hitting things and stopping", which is the challenging part of piloting a boat. That's made even more difficult when you're rusty or inexperienced.

This is why, no matter what else is happening on the water, you're guaranteed an exciting episode of Harbour Cinema almost every night.

***

Of course, one of the issues with Harbour Cinema is that it doesn't just constrain itself to cocktail hour. We were anchored on the town quay in Porto Cheli, waiting for another storm to pass us by. We learnt quickly that if you want a spot on a quay, you should arrive early. In the case of bad weather, we will often come a day or two earlier than needed simply because we can.

It was about 2 am one morning when I woke up to loud voices and *Matilda* moving side to side, along with an engine revving. I went onto the deck and saw a massive 15-metre (ca. 50 ft) catamaran trying to force its way into the gap between us and the next boat. The crew lined its decks, jamming fenders down the side, pushing on our safety rails as they tried to move us sideways and force their way in.

"What the fuck do you think you're doing!" The adrenaline had kicked in, and I went from zero to one hundred in seconds.

"Just release your stern line," replied the skipper. "We can slide in here!"

At 2 am, the last thing I wanted to be doing was adjusting my lines after we'd been in this position for a couple of days.

Karina was awakened by the shouting and came up to the deck, only to find me staring at the other skipper. As she told the story later, she could hear my shouting and assumed something was wrong. She fed off the energy and immediately started telling them to "Go away! You can't do this; go anchor out there! Don't damage my boat."

The skipper just continued to insist that he could fit.

"Mate, this is our boat — you can't just go banging around and damaging us with your charter. Get out of here!" I cried.

The skipper, who had been reasonably calm in the face of our aggression, now seemed to take offence.

"It's not a charter boat! This is my boat! We've been travelling for 36 hours straight; we need a space," he cried in a thick Russian accent. It seems one of the worst insults you can make is telling a boat owner they look like a charter.

They proceeded to ignore us and continued to try to fit the impossible square peg into a round hole. As Karina continued to tell them off from the bow of *Matilda*, I suddenly needed to walk away. I could feel I was ready to explode, the blood pounding through my head, and I wasn't making good decisions.

"Wait!" I yelled. "Give me a moment. I need to think."

I stormed along the quay, walking quickly to burn off some energy. By the time I reached the end, some 500 metres away, I had decided they were probably right. If I just loosened the stern line, they might be able to fit between us and the boat next door. With the way town quays work in Greece, as boats come and go, odd spaces get left behind — there's generally no one formally organising things and keeping everyone tucked in close.

Having cooled down, I returned to the boat and called out to the skipper.

"Ok. Here's the deal. I'm going to release the stern line. You can try again, but if that doesn't work — you can't stay; you have to go and anchor out there in the bay."

"OK, that's fair. Thank you," he replied.

It took less than a minute to add some slack into our lines, and while it was a tight fit, with fenders rubbing on both boats, they managed to reach the dock and successfully tie off.

When tempers had cooled the next morning, I figured I needed to try to make peace with the boat that would be our neighbours for the next few days.

"Thank you! This storm that's coming, it's going to be bad. We thought we'd outrun it and move here to be safe. I appreciate you helping us. We sailed 36 hours straight from the Ionian around the Peloponnese to get here," said the skipper.

As I chatted with Karina afterwards, we decided that there was a lesson there in empathy. If we'd been outrunning a storm for 36 hours, only to arrive in a port in the middle of the night, we'd be grateful if someone could just loosen their stern line by a metre so we could find shelter, too.

While there are other ways the catamaran could have approached the challenge (including just anchoring in the harbour, which is both large and safe), we'd certainly rather be known as helpful instead of obstructive.

You never really know what journey someone has gone through to get to where they are. We've yet to meet a boat problem that could be solved by more yelling[1]. Practising empathy, even when you disagree with what someone is trying to do, has always proven to be a more successful strategy.

***

As a novice skipper, it's easy to feel like everyone is watching what you're up to. That's because they are! If you would rather not feature in the latest blockbuster, it's good to know that the "classic hits" are easy to avoid.

Even the most experienced skippers can be undone by an inexperienced crew. While you may know precisely what you're doing, most crew are family or friends who've rarely been on a boat. At best, they are excited to be here, over-eager to help, and creating absolute havoc. At worst, they are entirely indifferent and regretting ever stepping aboard.

The majority of issues that happen during Harbour Cinema stem from two fundamental problems.

1. Setting and handling the stern lines.

2. Dropping (and setting) the anchor correctly.

Conceptually, number one is basic. When the boat reverses in, toss the line to someone on the shore, they wrap it around — or thread it through — something on the shore, then throw it back. You then tie the line off on the boat, all secured!

---

1. The exception to this rule is trying to unstick something. Yelling and swearing almost always helps in this case.

In practice, a new skipper will ask an inexperienced crew member to help with the lines. The crew member looks at the line and then loops one end (which is usually already tied into a loop) over a cleat on the deck in front of them. This is bad. Now, when they throw the line to shore, it travels OVER the lifelines, which can potentially bend or break them, damaging the boat.

That's assuming that the crew member can even throw the lines correctly. Often, novice sailors faced with the task of throwing a line to shore grab a big bundle that tangles midair, dropping into the water.

It creates all sorts of drama to watch. The people assisting on the shore yell to the crew that the lines are set wrong; the crew fail to understand and throws the armful of lines overboard anyway. Now, there are lines in the water, and the skipper is yelling at the crew because they're worried about snagging the propellor.

If the line does end up back on the boat, the skipper now suddenly has to dance between the helm and the ropes because no one on the crew knows how to tie off a cleat.

Spending five minutes training the crew before you arrive, and all these problems disappear. Show the crew how to set the lines properly (over the lifeline and loop the cleat from the outside of the boat) and how to flake[2] the rope onto the deck, then pick up three loops to toss it.

A deck cleat knot is simple to tie, but the crew don't even need to know that — they just need to know how to put a few quick loops around the cleat and use it for mechanical advantage. Then, the skipper can take their time to come around and tie things properly. But of course, cocktail hour would be a lot less interesting if this happened.

In reality (as long as the propellor doesn't get snagged), most of this drama is just noisy and relatively harmless.

The second issue of correctly setting the anchor is more concerning, and many a boat's been damaged by smacking into the dock because it hasn't been done correctly.

If they do think ahead, an inexperienced skipper usually places their most experienced person on the lines and puts the least experienced crew member (occasionally a child) up on the anchor to control the windlass remote. After all, that's straightforward: there are two buttons — up and down.

---

2. Pay the line out into a pile on the deck so it won't tangle and runs freely when thrown.

The problem is that the crew member up on the bow inevitably has no idea what they are trying to achieve, and, anyway, they can't hear the skipper shouting to drop the anchor.

When they finally get the message and start letting it out, they stop and start, all while the boat reverses toward the dock, wanting to check with the skipper that they are doing it right. Now, instead of a good 40–50 metres (ca. 130–150 ft.) of chain in front of the boat, there are maybe 15–20 metres (ca. 50-60 ft.). Nowhere near enough.

They are also terrified of the boat hitting the shore, so they fail to allow enough chain out for the boat to move closer to the dock. When the skipper yells at them to let out more chain, confused, they often bring it in. This drags the boat further away, making it more challenging for the crew to throw the lines and increasing the chances they will land in the water.

What should happen is that the next most experienced person is in the bow, controlling the anchor. They need explicit instruction to watch the skipper and not the scenery. The skipper needs to ensure the boat is brought to a halt when the anchor starts dropping, and then enough chain is released so that the anchor hits the bottom before reversing. They should release enough to set the anchor securely, then once the anchor has been tested to make sure it's holding, continue to reverse into the dock. The crew member on the bow continues to let more chain out as they go.

These issues are simple enough to avoid; even when they happen, it's rarely a big problem. Inexperienced crew panic and rush on boats because the environment is unfamiliar. But, in most cases, the worst that happens is bumping fenders with the boat next door. Maybe you hit the dock with the stern of the boat (which on charter boats is often covered with rubber for this reason). The worst case is you have to pull up the anchor and reset because it failed to set or there's not enough chain to hold the bow.

It's all embarrassing, but it's generally not an actual issue.

***

This is the backdrop of Harbour Cinema, the "Golden Oldies" that are rebroadcast day in and day out. You'll find us there on the end of the dock, ready to catch the line and, depending on how stressed and out of control things were, prepared to ask, "Captain, would you like some advice?"

Typically, we hear a grateful yes. People are usually willing to learn how to improve their technique. If we see the same skipper again later that week in a different port, we'll wave encouragement.

The bookend of each week's episodes is always on a Sunday or Friday when all the charter skippers set off for the week or start to cram into the one port to be ready to return to base on Saturday.

Charter boats all set off together and return to base on the same days. It means that the ports that are a predictable distance from popular charter bases get busy at the same time.

A typical example is the port of Hydra, which is very popular and incredibly small. It leads to four or five charter boats at a time circling inside a tiny harbour, trying to find a non-existent place to dock. But they can't circle; they need to do a three-point turn to get out again, and it's bedlam. Most experienced skippers won't go near Hydra at all, instead choosing the nearby port of Ermioni or anchoring on the mainland to catch a ferry to the island.

Imagine a car parking lot on the last shopping day before Christmas or during the Black Friday sales, and that's the chaos in ports everywhere in Greece during the peak charter season. Every so often, the cinema turns from a bumbling slapstick comedy to a dramatic action thriller.

In one memorable instance, a skipper reversing in strong winds missed the gap between the two boats. Instead of simply pulling forward and reversing again, they continued trying to reverse, trying to force the boat sideways. They then backed onto the chain of the boat next to them, which promptly wrapped their propellor and seized the engine.

In thirty seconds, ten skippers were standing on the edge of the dock, all offering to help. A hierarchy quickly emerged, with suggestions flowing up to the professional Greek skipper from a large charter boat, who knew what they were doing.

Fenders were procured and tied to the boat whose chain had been caught and loosened to help free it and prevent it from taking damage on the dock. A spare anchor was taken by tender out to the windward side of the boat in trouble, dropped and then tied back to its bow, creating a kedge[3] to hold it in place against the winds. Several people jumped in to dive and try to untangle the propellor, while others contacted the local professional diver, who eventually came out and was able to free it.

---

3. An anchor that's placed off to the side of a boat.

The point is that there's typically little that can be done from shore sitting back and watching a boat create problems for itself besides taking a drink and learning, ensuring that next time, it's not you in that situation. But when action can be taken, you'll find everyone willing to step in and help because we've all been there before.

Occasionally, you become the centre of attention yourself. One evening, we'd dropped anchor in a small sheltered bay with a pier on one side and cliffs on the other. We were towards the cliffs in an excellent sandy patch and felt secure.

The next day, the Coast Guard came around and announced a cruise ship would be arriving and moved several boats anchored near us. They never asked us to move, so we presumed we'd be fine. Which we were, but early the next morning, we were jolted awake by the sound of a giant chain letting go off the rear of *Matilda*.

I popped up to see a small cruise ship, about 50 metres (ca. 160 ft) in length, dropping its anchor roughly 3 metres (ca. 10 ft) behind us. Apart from watching, there wasn't much I could do as it backed down and docked at the shore. While they were close, there was no danger of our anchors getting tangled as they were secured to the dock, and we were already at the end of our swing, so we were not going to get any closer.

We thought nothing more of it until later; we had dinner with friends who were also anchored there with us. They'd been hiking when the cruise ship came in and took photos that showed just how close the ship came to us. It looked much more dramatic from their vantage point up the hill.

We were definitely that day's episode of Harbour Cinema and hadn't even realised it.

***

The other Harbour Cinema classic is a problem exacerbated by the stern-to mooring common in the Mediterranean. Crossed anchor chains.

In a perfect world, everyone drops their anchor directly in front of the position on the dock where their boat will tie to. In reality, many skippers frequently miss the mark. Maybe the crew member on the anchor didn't understand the instructions. Perhaps the wind is blowing strongly across the harbour. Whatever the reason, the anchor has dropped a few boats over from where they eventually tie off. Now, their anchor chain is lying over the top of the chain of all those other boats. In theory, if the person who came in last leaves first, everything should be fine, but in practice, it never happens that way.

One of the boats that had its chain crossed may not even realise it occurred. They wake up early, excited about a day of cruising, and try to leave. As they try to lift their chain, it slides under the chain of the boat that crossed it. If they keep pulling up the chain, eventually, it will hook onto the flukes of the anchor that crossed it and lift it out of the water.

For the boat that caused the issue by dropping over the anchor chains, the sound of their chain being lifted creates a loud rumbling sound through the hull. The skipper who created the chaos comes running to the bow, shouting at the boat that's attempting to leave, "You've hooked my anchor".

This, while true, also ignores the fact they were the ones who caused the situation in the first place.

The departing boat is unable to get free. Unsure of what to do, they now take the anchor they've hooked for a walk around the port[4]. Helpful people on the dock yell instructions that can't be heard in the wind while the boat circles. With luck, they will eventually free their chain, dropping the anchor they lifted on the spot they released from it, which crosses yet more anchors and causes more problems for other boats planning to leave.

With the boat that wanted to leave out of the way, now the boat that had its anchor lifted is in trouble. As their anchor is no longer set, they start to drift back toward the dock. Panicking, they start their motors and release their stern lines. With luck, they exit without catching a line in a prop. Then, as they haul their chain in, their anchor drags over the chains of other boats, and the flukes catch on yet another chain, and the whole drama begins again.

While it would be preferable that everyone dropped their anchor perfectly, this never happens. It's anything but a perfect world when docking in a strange harbour with winds gusting. Crossed anchors happen... a lot.

It's not really the fault of the skippers. There are three types of skippers when it comes to crossing anchors: those who have, those who have yet to, and those who've lied about it. You learn how to deal with it through experience or chatting with others who've had the experience. Every sailing course I've taken has been sadly lacking in teaching you what to do when you've just turned your boat into a giant fishing pole and hooked a 10+ tonne boat on the other end of your chain.

---

4. To quote Monster's Inc. "Put that thing back where it came from, or so help me!"

The irony, of course, is that the boat that is stuck on the chain is usually perfectly safe while stuck. They are on a floating object that can't move other than spinning around its fixed point. In other words, they are at anchor. With fenders ready, there's no real risk to the crew or other boats.

What's especially challenging is that the skipper who initially caused the mess is the one who can solve it easily. But they don't know how. Counter-intuitively, they need to immediately start their motor to move forward while still tied to the dock, then release more chain. This will hold them in place, allowing the boat that's stuck enough slack in the chain to lift it and free themselves.

With slack on the chain, the boat trying to leave can raise its anchor to deck level. They then attach a rope to the stuck chain, lower their anchor again, and the chain stays up, and the anchor falls down. They are now free to depart. The boat still tied to shore, tightens its chain again, and that's it. Problem solved.

Sadly, most novice skippers aren't familiar with this process, so instead of dealing effectively with the issue, they deliver an entertaining session of Harbour Cinema. And we get to learn a lot of colourful new swear words in foreign languages.

Ultimately, Harbour Cinema is a big part of the cruising experience. Everyone has a tale to tell of the time they watched some skipper make a fundamental mistake and a story or two of the times that skipper was them. There's no doubt in my mind that Harbour Cinema has been amusing sailors since the first Neanderthal set off to explore in a hollowed-out log.

Eleven

Confidence

"I'm not afraid of storms, for I'm learning how to sail my ship." — Louisa May Alcott

At some point, no matter how much of a novice you feel, you'll hopefully have a moment of realisation that perhaps you do, in fact, know something after all. That all the experience, the failures, and the challenges you've faced to get to where you are today actually meant something.

It starts small. We might be chatting with a charter boat anchored nearby, and they mention they are heading to Ermioni.

"Oh nice, we love Ermioni! If you're there, definitely take the small ferry that leaves from the north side to go and visit Hydra. And if you're stern-to on the south, be sure to put out a lot of chain; you'll be dropping in 15 metres. Make sure you visit Drougas; it's the best bakery in the area." You rattle off this information without thinking about it.

As we continued to cruise around the Argolic and Saronic Gulfs, slowly exploring new ports and harbours, we began to find ourselves one of the more experienced cruisers. Even when we'd meet someone with vastly more experience, they valued the local knowledge of someone who was "just there".

I've caught the lines for a very nervous first-time captain who struggled, along with his crew, to get his charter boat successfully moored stern-to in the port of Aegina. A second boat was still circling and having issues, and I joked with him, "Don't worry, you're 100% more experienced than that skipper now!"

Later that week, I spotted the same captain attempting to moor stern-to in much more challenging conditions. The wind was blowing strong, the swell was pushing the boats around even inside the harbour, and getting the boat set in the correct position was hard. It took him two or three tries to get it right, but the boat was always under control, and he eventually managed to drop the anchor in the right spot.

As I took the line, he recognised me and said, "No worries, I'm more experienced now than that guy," pointing at the next boat struggling to set their anchor and moor.

Everything you do builds knowledge, good and bad. Every day, you find yourself increasing in confidence:

- Confidence in the crew. Karina and I now know much more about what we're doing and have established processes and procedures for all the regular situations we encounter.

- Confidence in the boat. Every big wave crossing, every strong gust, gives us increased confidence in what *Matilda* can handle.

- Perhaps most importantly, it is having confidence in yourself. As a skipper, cautious confidence is one of the best tools you can have on board.

When everything goes well, and it usually does, you'll have outstanding experiences that make it all worthwhile.

But when the unexpected happens, confidence that it will be okay is essential, too. The weather will turn when you weren't planning for it. Systems will break, and something will leak that isn't meant to. That's just cruising. Well-founded confidence means that you'll take it in your stride and keep moving forward, that you've prepared the boat, the crew and yourself so that you have a plan regardless of what comes your way.

With two months in the same region completed, our boat licenses squared away, and plenty of things broken and repaired again[1], we were becoming confident. We felt like we had this whole liveaboard boat thing under control. It was time to start heading further afield and to strike out for somewhere more ambitious, to brave the dreaded Meltemi and explore the Cyclades.

***

---

1. Frequently more than once!

There are rare individuals in the world who have all the skills required to sail on a cruising boat. They are rigging experts, they are diesel mechanics, they are electricians with expertise in battery chargers and solar-powered systems. They can build a watermaker from scratch with a tin can and a piece of kitchen sponge. Not only that, but they could MacGyver up a new autopilot system from some old stainless and a torn piece of rope. And then there's the rest of us. Making it up as we go along.

I most regularly meet this type of expert online. Instead of out there travelling, they are sitting back in a cruising forum or Facebook group, dispensing advice, disparaging others and making it seem like you'd be insane to spend more than five minutes on board a boat without knowing how to service the engine and clean the fuel injectors with nothing but pliers and a piece of used dental floss. In practice, in the real world, the more experienced the sailor I meet, the more likely you'll hear "I don't know", even when they know everything and more.

Of course, an excellent foundational knowledge of the systems aboard your boat is important, but it also really depends on what you plan to do. If you're crossing the Pacific, literally weeks away from land and even further from the technical support to fix what's wrong, then you need a good set of spares on board and the knowledge of how to use them.

But if you're like the vast majority of cruisers — coastal cruisers like ourselves – you're rarely more than an hour or two from a safe harbour and access to skilled support.

That's not saying it isn't good to be able to fix things yourself; generally speaking, it's (usually) cheaper, and it's absolutely one of the satisfying parts of owning a boat. The point is, you don't have to. If there are some things that you don't understand, it's still far better to get out there and experience the cruising lifestyle. At least, it's better than sitting through hours of courses on the fundamentals of how to service a marine air conditioner unless that's your thing.

So, if you don't have to be a mechanical savant to safely undertake a life coastal cruising the Mediterranean or even to cross the Atlantic, what is the essential skill you need to have?

I think it's confidence. You don't have to know how to fix everything, but you do need to be able to work out roughly what's broken. You must know how to assess and manage the risk appropriate to your boat and what you plan to do.

As we prepared to tackle the Cyclades, heading further away from our familiar lo-cations and resources, we ran through the current state of things on *Matilda*. Yes, the freshwater tank was still leaking, but since starting the season, we'd replaced the engine batteries, had the motors checked, upgraded all the electronics, repaired the canvas and much, much more. We were in great shape to set off and explore further afield. There were potentially things that could go wrong, but we felt confident that we could manage them if they did.

When planning a passage, it's important to stay realistic about the problems that could occur and the plans you put in place. Yes, it's possible that you could get struck by a meteor, but this is so unlikely it's not worth worrying about.

There's also a series of things that can go wrong that, while inconvenient, don't impact the boat or crew's safety. For example, if the water tank were to fail, we could flush the heads[2] by bucket and drink bottled water, which is readily available everywhere in Greece.

This leads to the point that risk is also very individual. For us, a failed water tank is an inconvenience, but if you're crossing the Atlantic at sea for twenty days or more, the failure of a water tank might be critical.

More realistic risks are dangerous things like collisions with the land or other boats. These sorts of risks are reduced with good planning. It's mitigated by choosing good weather conditions to cruise in and familiarising yourself with charts and navigation rules. Keeping a good watch is essential (Rule 5[3]), and tools like chart plotters, GPS, AIS[4], and radar make it even easier.

With that said, collisions with other boats do happen. In Greece, the waters are crowded with inexperienced charterers, aggressive tour boat operators and tiny unmarked fishing vessels. Still, the risk of collision has always felt like a small one and not something we've been too concerned about. We plan, prepare, use the tools available to us, obey the rules and then stay the heck out of the way if we're not happy with how things are shaping up. In reality, most collisions happen at low speeds in harbours — more likely to do minor damage to your boat than sink it.

The scariest risks are the ones you can't plan for when previously reliable things break down and potentially impact the boat's safety at sea. The most realistic of these risks on *Matilda* is probably an engine failure. Marine diesel engines are incredibly reliable. The

---

2. Boats are full of strange words for very average things. The toilet.

3. Colregs Rule 5 - Every vessel shall at all times maintain a proper lookout by sight and hearing.

4. The automatic identification system, or AIS, transmits a ship's position so that other ships can see it on an electronic chart.

risk of one failing once you're underway is small, but it's a possibility. You could have lousy fuel, an impellor[5] could fail, and the engine overheat, or perhaps something more major goes wrong.

The most obvious way this risk is managed is an alternative source of propulsion – something that's a requirement under various national flag rules throughout the Mediterranean. If you have a sailboat, then this alternate propulsion is the engine (or, more realistically, the sails are the alternate to the engine[6]). For us on *Matilda*, our backup is our second engine. If one engine were to fail catastrophically, we'd still have the other and be able to limp back to port. To back that up, we've got the onboard VHF radio and a hand-held VHF. There's also an EPIRB (Emergency Position Indicating Radio Beacon) and DSC (Digital Selective Calling[7]) to send distress calls. We have flares and light signalling devices. If both engines failed for some reason in the Mediterranean, we could contact someone to get assistance.

I'm not very knowledgeable about diesel engines beyond the basics of checking fluids, belts and impellors and how to resolve those if needed. But for what we're doing, I don't really need to be. We've mitigated the risk with the second engine. We have a second fallback (a way to contact people). There's a third emergency contact fallback (EPIRB, DSC and flares) and a fourth option (an onboard tender and a life raft if we had to abandon ship for some reason).

Most importantly, as this is one of the most significant risks we face, we invest the money to ensure the engines are properly maintained. We pay for quality maintenance from certified mechanics. With two well-maintained engines in good condition that are well cared for, we feel confident in setting forth on longer passages. We know we've got the redundancy required for even the most extreme circumstances.

***

---

5. Usually made from hard rubber. It has fins, like the spokes on a wheel. The fins can break off at annoying times and water will stop flowing through the pump.

6. They say MED stands for Motor Every Day.

7. DSC can be used for many things, but the most relevant here is to broadcast an automated distress call containing your GPS coordinates at the touch of a button.

With confidence in ourselves and *Matilda* at a high, we set off from Aegina, leaving what we were coming to consider our "home port" to head for the small harbour of Agias Niklaus[8], on the south side of the mainland, just before Cape Sounion. We anchored there overnight and then, with a favourable weather window, headed for the island of Kea early the following day.

Passing Cape Sounion is one of the highlights of any sailor's experience. As you cruise beneath the imposing cliffs that tower above you, the Temple of Poseidon sits there, an ancient homage to the god of the sea. Even the least superstitious among us will say a quiet word, asking for a safe passage. At that moment, you could be 2,000 years in the past. It's easy to imagine that if you glanced into the bay sheltered beneath the temple, you could see the mighty triremes of the ancient Athenian fleet. They used this bay as a staging point to help enforce their dominance on the surrounding islands.

And then you look back south, and you're snapped back to the reality of modern Greece, huge ferries and colossal container ships plying their way from Athens off the coast, heading for the islands and further points unknown.

We arrived at the Kea without any issues and successfully tied stern-to after a couple of attempts. It was a rude reminder of the value of local knowledge. We picked a convenient-looking place on the quay, only to discover that it was empty because an underwater shelf was jutting out that prevented us from reaching the dock. So we hauled anchor, picked another spot and reset.

From Kea, we turned south for the next island in the chain, Kithnos, but on the eastern side this time. Scarred by the memory of our first overnight trip to Kolonos Beach, we decided to avoid it and explore new harbours instead. After a few days in the small port of Loutra, we skipped down the coast and crossed the busy shipping channel to anchor in a large, deserted bay on the northern side of the island of Serifos.

The tourist season was gradually coming to a close, and the facilities were shutting down. The organised beach was empty, the taverna boarded up, and everything eerily quiet after the more populated areas we'd been going through. Instead of hordes of charter boats, other liveaboards and activity in towns, we were now isolated by ourselves. For the first time I can recall on *Matilda*, we were utterly alone in a bay.

The isolation felt even more complete when we woke up the following day. The sea was un-naturally calm, and a dense sea fog, the thickest in over thirty years, had descended on

8. Greek for Saint Nicholas, also the patron saint of sailors (and Father Christmas).

the islands overnight. It was sitting just outside the bay, a wall of white that prevented us from seeing anything at all.

We debated what to do, but with the wind switching to the north, we decided we'd be better off moving to the island's southern side as planned the night before. It meant venturing into the wall of fog, but we were confident, we were prepared, and we set out!

As we cruised out of the bay, the fog got thicker and thicker until we could barely see the bow of *Matilda* in front of us. The air was surprisingly damp; our hair started to drip from the water catching on it. Fortunately, we have a good chart plotter with an up-to-date map, so we "flew by wire", mainly navigating based on our position on the screen. We started the radar, which, from experience, has been reliable at identifying fishing boats, the most significant risk in this weather. I also checked the navigation on my phone as a backup. With our lights on and regularly sounding our horns, we continued forth.

The fog never lifted in the two hours it took us to reach the main town. Later that day, we hiked up to the top of the hill and the chora (main town), which sits up with a fantastic view over the surroundings in the centre of Serifos. The sky was a brilliant blue, but everywhere below about 50 metres was covered in a blanket of thick white, the peaks of the nearby island of Sifnos sticking up in the distance.

The next day, it cleared, and we headed to Sifnos, then the island of Milos, where we planned to spend a few days exploring and waiting out some big winds coming through.

***

We were proud of ourselves. We'd made it through the Western Cyclades to Milos with minimal fuss. The one curveball, the heavy fog, had been navigated without issue, and we'd arrived in time to position ourselves ready for the weather.

We weren't the only other sailors with the good idea of waiting out the weather in Milos. There was an interesting group of four other boats, all holed up from the same storm. Our confidence, which had been soaring sky-high in our abilities to explore safely by sea, took a dent as we realised just how much more we had to learn compared to them.

Perhaps the most seasoned sailor there was Martin, who had circumnavigated the world several times. Among most sailors, circumnavigation is regarded as a bit of a big deal. He described it simply as "There's no magic, I'm just stubborn... and lucky." after a bit more thought, he added, "And I have a lot of time."

Stubbornness, as Martin said, goes a long way. More specifically, though, I think it's a form of confidence. You don't have to know how to fix everything, but you do need to be able to work out roughly what's broken. You have to understand how to assess and manage the risk appropriate to your boat and what you're planning to do.

Martin is typical of most experienced sailors I've met. Humble and understated, with the knowledge that no matter how much you know, there's always more to learn from the most unexpected places. Unlike the online experts, the experienced sailors out there doing it are almost always encouraging. They remember what it's like to be faced with something you don't understand — perhaps as recently as the day before! And they know that it's the lived experience that helps you to grow. They won't pull punches – if you do something stupid, they'll tell you. But they ultimately want to see you safe and out there, enjoying the world and exploring by sea. They aren't gatekeepers but enablers.

Then there was Rob, who had a beautiful wooden boat, around 40 years old, which he'd purchased and then restored in Türkiye over several years. A clearly capable sailor, his goals were clear. He wanted to return his boat to the shipyard that built it in the UK. He felt it was of value that the boat completed its circumnavigation, which it had made most of the way before being abandoned in Türkiye, and that the yard would appreciate seeing their work restored. It's a sentiment we appreciate. Does it really matter if the boat returned to the yard that built it? Probably not, but Rob understood that boats have a soul and there's a special kind of romance and magic in undertaking an adventure at sea "just because."

Finally, we met Philipp and Klim, two young sailors who were solo sailing across the Mediterranean for the pure adventure of it. They were approaching it in very different ways, Philipp with the meticulous preparation that is stereotypically German, while Klim, a Russian, was taking a more "fly by the seat of his pants" approach. It was epitomised in an exchange between them as the weather lifted.

"My headlamp broke! Does anyone know where I can buy a new one?" Klim asked.

"Here, you can take this one; it's my spare," replied Philipp.

"But I don't want to take your only spare!"

"Don't worry. I have two."

We found them both inspirational young men, 19 and 20 years of age, exploring in small 7-metre (ca. 24 ft) boats. They showed us that confidence and the desire to get out there and explore will take you a long way and that preparation doesn't always mean spending much money.

There's no doubt that money is important, but Philipp and Klim showed us that there's a way to live this lifestyle without it, too. It's fair to point out that at just over 50 years old, Karina and I have acquired a reasonable amount of assets, and we also expect a certain level of comfort. Not necessarily luxury, but we appreciate the creature comforts a bigger boat brings, like a washing machine, a separate shower cubicle and a proper-sized double bed. Still, when it comes to safety and ability, you can cruise the Mediterranean on a lot less.

It was an unexpected lesson in our first season, but an important one: there's always someone with a bigger boat. It doesn't matter how well off or not you are; boating attracts some very wealthy people.

Own a modern boat built within the last few years? There's someone who has one they commissioned new this year.

Are you proud of your blue-water-capable catamaran? Here comes someone with the latest performance cat with a carbon fibre rig.

Are you the envy of your friends on your 15-metre (ca. 50 ft) mono hull? Pull into the marina, and you're surrounded by bigger 18-metre (ca. 60 ft) boats.

Own a 35-metre (ca. 115 ft) superyacht? The marina we wintered at in Montenegro at the end of our second season is home to two boats, each over 100 metres (ca. 328 ft) in length. They still aren't the biggest privately owned boats in the world. No matter where you sit on the spectrum, there's always someone with something newer, faster, bigger or prettier.

It doesn't mean that you want all of that. I know enough now to recognise that not only is *Matilda* very comfortable for us, but we couldn't begin to afford the berth and maintenance fees on a much bigger boat. Still, a certain level of jealousy is allowed.

The point is, if you accept that there will always be someone with a better boat, you can start to get on with being proud of what you have. And, sometimes, you might realise that you need less than you think.

Philipp, in his 7-metre (ca. 24 ft) sailing boat *Tamata* shared the same quay, views, and experience as us in Milos. He's an inspirational example of just getting out there and doing it. He'd just turned 20 years old and had already been solo sailing and exploring in the Mediterranean for a couple of months. His boat *Tamata*, a "trailer sailor"[9], is an old

---

9. Quite literally, a sail boat small enough to be towed by a trailer on the road.

Danish design from 1973 with a full heavy keel. She's a capable blue water sailor despite her tiny size.

As we were holed up from the weather, we spent time with Philipp and Klim travelling around Milos, and Philipp shared more of his story. He first found *Tamata* on eBay as a project boat; the previous owner had stripped it down and then decided the restoration was too much effort. They came to a deal. Phillip, then just 18 and at the start of his penultimate year of high school, would buy the trailer. The boat? That would be free — in exchange for pictures once the restoration was complete.

Over the next two years, Philipp taught himself how to rebuild or remake every part of the boat. He wired in all the electronics and rebuilt and refinished all the wood. He refitted the galley and put in batteries and solar, all because he dreamed of sailing from Slovenia to the island of Rhodes in Greece by himself as soon as he finished high school.

Bit by bit, he pieced the boat back together, completing school while he took the time to learn from friends and neighbours the skills he needed to make the boat restoration happen. After much hard work, it was eventually ready to launch. He took it to his local lake, where he practised sailing and underwent sea trials. After a few final modifications, he was prepared to go.

With his father's help, he towed the boat to Slovenia, finally launching it into the Adriatic Sea. He spent another week completing a further shakedown with Dad onboard as crew, then he waved farewell and, at the age of 19, set off solo cruising to Rhodes.

By the time we met in Milos, he'd just completed a 20-hour crossing from Monemvasia at his cruising speed of only 4.5 knots using a tiny outboard motor.

While Karina and I wouldn't be touring the Mediterranean full-time on his boat, the point of the story is that with minimal resources and a little luck, he's out there living his dream.

As an outsider, it's easy to look at Philipp on his tiny boat and see a lack of resources; after all, why would you voluntarily cruise on something so small? But he and his boat are rich in capabilities in every way that matters. If something were to break, he not only had a complete set of spares but the skill to repair most things — after all, he rebuilt the whole boat himself.

When we told him we were horrified at the thought of Tamata dealing with the large swells that forced us all into Milos, he shrugged and said, "It's easier for me; she's so short she just slips between the waves, not crashing through them like you."

He knows and appreciates the value of what he has, and it's letting him get out there and live the dream, which, as it turns out, is really step one of a much larger plan. Once the crossing to Rhodes was completed, his goal was to attend merchant navy school and become an officer on cargo ships.

After completing his initial training in Germany, he planned to return to Rhodes and sail back to Slovenia, where he'd take the boat by trailer to the harbour near his college. There, he wants to live on his boat, saving money so that after he graduates, he can afford an aluminium-hulled ketch to circumnavigate the world "without cheating," as he puts it. This means he intends to take the challenging route, cruising past the Great Capes (Cape of Good Hope, Cape Horn and Cape Leeuwin) instead of using the Panama and Suez canals.

He's now more than twelve months into his merchant navy career and doing practical training on cargo ships; I have no doubt he'll achieve his goals and cruise the world in his aluminium boat. The last time I checked, he was on holiday, crossing the South Pacific on a friend's boat, racking up yet more experience on his way to his dream.

While there's some luck along the way, it's more about grit, determination and confidence you can succeed than anything else. You could pick up a similar project boat in less disarray than Philipp's started at for a few thousand euros at most. While he had a leg up, it wasn't a huge one.

Maybe your ambition is a bigger boat. Even if your reality (like ours) is a desire for a more comfortable bed and a bit more space on board, we can all learn a lesson from the benefits of focused motivation and the confidence to make the dream happen. Ultimately, the difference in who ends up cruising is between dreamers and doers. Philipp spent less time reading internet forums and more time invested in working on a boat and getting it afloat.

Milos was a transformational step for us on our boating journey. It was the first time that we truly started to feel a part of the liveaboard community and that we belonged. Beyond experience, the most critical skill is confidence and getting out there. In the act of being there, you, too, are doing and living the life and gaining skills. We'd found our tribe no longer "just cruisers" but part of a tradition and community that spans the globe—a community of adventurers.

Twelve

Challenge

"The fishermen know that the sea is dangerous and the storm terrible, but they have never found these dangers sufficient reason for remaining ashore." —Vincent Van Gogh

The inevitable consequence of confidence is overconfidence. With every successful night at anchor and each completed crossing, we continued gaining confidence in ourselves and *Matilda*. Eventually, we were bound to either push too hard or something was going to break. Hopefully, not both.

One area of weakness for me starting this adventure was blind faith in weather prediction apps. I think it has something to do with my background in technology. I tend to expect computers to give black-and-white answers. In reality, weather prediction is complex, nuanced, and frequently just wrong.

At the scale that weather operates, a prediction can be correct overall but just plain wrong at the local level. If you place the edge of a weather front a mere 5 km out of place, that's probably a damn good prediction when you're predicting weather for the whole of Greece. For the boat seeking a safe harbour, it could mean a rough night.

Local conditions play havoc in other ways. The overall prediction might be for the air mass to move south at roughly 10 knots, but right here, the landscape creates a funnel in the channel between two islands, and the wind blows a lot stronger.

Which is precisely where we found ourselves on our first rough crossing. We had left Milos as our brief fellowship all went our separate ways, spreading out over the Aegean Sea.

We'd crossed to the island of Anti-Paros and were now heading north, between the islands of Paros and Naxos, to get to Naxos port to meet our friend Erik. It started okay, but as we headed further up the channel, the waves were growing and starting to crash up and over the bow of the boat — the first time we'd really experienced that.

Having failed to account for the landscape, we found the wind gusting much stronger than predicted. It left us with no great choices to make. We could turn back, press on, or head somewhere else.

Turning back didn't make sense, as we were almost halfway to Naxos port anyway, and the wind had picked up since we left. If we headed back south, the waves and wind would still be there, increasing, but now following us, which is undesirable as the waves get bigger.

We could abort. Just give in and head sideways to a nearby port. This wasn't an option as the waves are far worse when we take them side on, and anyway, none of the nearby ports looked to be that sheltered from the wind and the increasing swell.

So press on it was. We're committed, and the best course was to continue forward. We turned slightly off our route to "quarter" the waves. Now we're heading slightly sideways to them, no longer ploughing directly over and crashing down, but riding up and over them, sliding through the trough. It meant a longer journey but a safer feeling one.

Doors started to fly open as things moved in cupboards. Heavy toolboxes that had remained safely stored for the last four months crashed through the cupboard doors and over the floor, spilling tools and creating havoc and noise.

We tried heading closer to shore, where the coast of Naxos curving west towards Paros protected us from the swell building up. That worked for a time, but eventually, we had to exit through the north end of the channel and cut across the swell to Naxos port. For the last hour, we were fully exposed to the large waves rolling down the Aegean, kicked up by the building Meltemi.

Unsure of exactly where the entrance to the port was and worried about the depths between a rocky outcrop and land, we took the longer route further out to sea. In hindsight, this still seems like the correct, safe decision, although it frustrated us at the time as we felt we were getting further away from our objective.

It's strange thinking back on it. Emotionally, I still feel that was the worst conditions we've experienced underway. They were undoubtedly stressful. But in reality, I suspect that we've since experienced worse—both bigger waves and stronger winds. After all, the benefit of experience is that, hopefully, you get better at it.

When we finally pulled into port, we initially entered the wrong harbour, an old ferry port on the north side of Naxos Town. It was quickly apparent that this was not where the private boats typically anchor, but finding shelter was such a relief that we sat there for thirty minutes, taking stock. We stowed the tools spread around the floor and settled our stomachs before heading back out for the ten minutes of chaos to get to the correct entrance.

It was a harsh lesson on weather prediction, and we're now much more cautious about reading the conditions. We spend more time considering what the weather is meant to do. We look at what we know of the landscape, what the weather was doing yesterday, and what we're actually experiencing right now. Not only that, but we no longer unquestioningly trust what's presented to us.

While I wouldn't willingly set out in those conditions again, it's not all bad. Having experienced them has helped us understand how *Matilda*, and her crew handle adverse weather. We now willingly head out in conditions that previously kept us trapped in port, as we know we're perfectly able to handle it.

***

Some people enjoy cruising at night; it can be incredibly peaceful and often much calmer in summer when coastal cruising. For many passages, or just because you need to make some distance, it's unavoidable.

I've not experienced enough of them to have a strong opinion, but let's say my impressions to date have been mixed. This is partly because the few night crossings we've done were forced on us, not a conscious decision on our part. When given the choice, we prefer the warmth of a summer day, enjoying the view, and arriving at an anchorage in daylight to pick a good spot.

We crossed from Naxos to Syros and continued waiting out the stormy weather, while our friend Hannah made the trip from Germany to Athens and then on the ferry to be with us. While we'd emphasised that our plans weren't exactly set in stone, we still felt a strong obligation to get her back to Aegina to meet a friend. The weather had other plans.

We set off from Syros to Kithnos, a crossing that was already a little challenging. The winds were strong on the side of the boat, and with winter rapidly approaching, the nights fell a lot earlier, and we crossed the last section in the dark.

But we'd made it and tucked ourselves back into the port of Loutra, where we'd been towards the start of our Cyclades adventures. There had been several days of strong northerly winds, and finally, the next night, there was a lull of around five hours when the wind was turning back to the south. A potential window for us to cross out of the Cyclades and back to Athens.

I cringe as I write this. There's so much wrong with this statement that experience has taught us the hard way. The idea we'd plan something with that degree of precision in the weather forecast is laughable now. But we had an open body of water to cross and a destination to reach. We were going to go for it.

Throughout the day, we'd headed to the top of a nearby ridge to watch the sea. I could tell that the wind was easing off. The spray whipping off the top of the waves was dissipating and settling down to regular "white horses" rolling across the sea. It looked like the forecast was correct; the wind was dropping, and we should be good to go.

As evening fell and the appointed window approached, we started preparing the boat. I switched on the navigation lights for the first time, only to find that the starboard light had failed. We had several spares on board, so a few moments of cursing and a skinned knuckle soon had the plastic case removed and the bulb replaced, only for the second globe to immediately fail, too. I replaced it again, and finally, the light was on. We've since replaced the older filament globes with LEDs that don't seem to fail (yet).

Another item has also made it to the maintenance checklists – I now check the navigation lights regularly, even when we're not planning a night passage. Of course, being a boat, none of that checking probably means anything! Guaranteed as soon as I actually need the navigation lights to work for real during the night, something will fail again, but it won't be for lack of preparation this time.

With everything in order, we reviewed the forecast again, conducted our final go-no-go poll,[1] started the motors and pulled out of the harbour. We headed north out of the port, intending to round the top of Kithnos, cross below the island of Kea, past Cape Sounion and then along the coast of the mainland to Agias Niklaus, the anchorage we'd stayed at previously.

The balmy summer evenings we'd become accustomed to had well and truly passed. Sitting in my usual position at the helm on the flybridge, the first thing that I was

---

1. While safety rests with the captain, in poor conditions, I want the crew to have a say too. I was confident but if anyone was concerned, we'd stay in port for another night.

unprepared for was just how cold it would be once the sun went down. The wind across the sea without the warmth from the sun was biting. That was easily fixed by adding on a few more layers. Karina and Hannah sat in the main cabin, warm inside, watching TV as we cruised along.

The second thing that surprised me was how dark it is at sea on a moonless night. We're so used to light pollution that the inky blackness of the sea at night is a surprise. It's awe-inspiring, majestic, magical and terrifying all at the same time.

With no visual frame of reference apart from a compass and chart plotter, you feel lost, adrift in the blackness, with the sound of the boat the only noise. It's a testament to the skills of the ancient navigators that they could navigate purely by the stars — the first sailors to set off beyond sight of the shores were brave beyond belief. And the skies that night were overcast; there were no stars to be seen.

After an hour cruising north in the dark, a series of lights appeared on the horizon ahead of me. At first, I thought it was a fishing vessel, but it seemed too dispersed for that. I saw one set of lights at the water line and another at mast height. I checked the radar and couldn't see anything showing, yet the lights kept tracking directly for me.

I veered about 25 degrees to starboard, thinking perhaps it was the lights on fish farms that I was seeing. After travelling for a few more minutes, the lights slowly came closer, not changing bearing at all. They still appeared to be heading straight at us.

I grabbed the binoculars, and suddenly, it became clear. What I'd confused with another boat, or perhaps a fish farm, was the lights of two towns about 15 nautical miles north of us on Kea. One cluster of lights was at the water's edge, and the other was higher up the cliff towards the top of the island. Far from an imminent collision, it would take almost two hours for us to reach them.

Now that I realised what it was, it also became apparent in plain sight. It was my first real introduction to the tricks the sea and the darkness can play on you at night.

Eventually, we rounded the top of Kithnos and headed westward through the passage between it and Kea. The swell started to pick up, and it began to rain. We'd left the shelter on the island's eastern side and were now exposed to the weather pushing down from the northwest. I retreated inside the main cabin to the master helm; trading reduced visibility for increased comfort and safety.

It isn't easy to know just how big the swell really was. We couldn't see the waves well enough in the pitch black, although many were crashing up and over the bow. They were at least 1–2 metres (ca. 3–6 feet), which isn't that big, but it's certainly uncomfortable.

The main problem was that they were hitting us on the beam, and without a horizon to spot, the rolling meant that everyone on board, including me, started to feel seasick.

Seasickness is a reality of boat life. Everyone experiences it at some point. You've either been seasick, or you're lying about it. After a season of cruising, we thought we were well on top of it. But, with the need to stay inside due to the weather, the constant rolling motion and the stress of travelling in the pitch black, we were on the verge of throwing up.

I managed to keep my stomach under control by opening the side door and sitting in the fresh air. It meant I now had the choice between staying warm and dry but feeling nauseous or feeling generally okay but cold, wet, and miserable. I ended up flipping back and forth between the two options. I stayed inside long enough to get warm until the nausea got too bad, then hung my head out the door until I couldn't stand the cold anymore, but my stomach felt fine.

When you have a guest on board, things that might be inconvenient dial up a notch. I knew the conditions made Hannah miserable, and felt terrible that it was my fault. It was my decisions as captain that had put us out here in poor conditions.

Still, she was a champion about it; despite the obvious nausea, she treated it all like part of the big adventure. With a long-term family history from the sea-faring port of Hamburg and her experiences sailing on the North Sea, she was embarrassed she wasn't handling it and was determined to put on a cheery face.

As we continued west, we left the shelter of Kea, and the swell started to pick up even more. It's hard to know what to do in these conditions — pressing on means that you've got another hour or so to go before finding shelter, but the conditions might get even worse. Turning back won't get you out of the conditions immediately, and we'd have two hours before we could round the corner and head south again back to Loutra.

We pressed on. Tired, sick and exhausted, we finally made it across the passage to the mainland of Greece. I waved a thank you to the Temple of Poseidon as we passed Cape Sounion. We'd made it, and while the crew had taken a battering, *Matilda* had handled it all with aplomb. With the mainland now sheltering us from the swell, we continued uneventfully along the coast to our target anchorage.

Then, it was time to anchor. It seems obvious now, but I'd never considered it before departing. Dropping anchor in the dark means you can't see where you're putting the anchor. We've resolved this problem now with a very high-powered LED torch, which we can use to see the bottom, but at the time, we had no idea where to drop.

While it wasn't immediately of use, the advice of more experienced sailors suddenly clicked into place in my head. This is why they leave at 2 am. It's far safer to arrive in a new port with the light than in the dark. The most significant danger on a boat isn't typically out at sea; it's when you're close to land. It's far better to arrive when you can see what you're doing in a strange harbour.

Fortunately, we were back in Agias Niklaus, where we'd stopped before crossing to the Cyclades, and at this time of year, there were no other boats. I knew where on the charts I'd dropped previously, so I positioned the boat as close to there as possible, then dropped the anchor and hoped. The anchor set first time, and with the wind continuing to fall and plenty of chain out, we all collapsed into our cabins to sleep away what was left of the night.

You don't know what you don't know. Despite the planning that had gone into the crossing, our practical experience of predicting the weather, and familiarity with our destination, we'd still found new things to surprise us and new lessons to learn.

***

Storm cells are another weather challenge that we, like many sailors, have learnt a lot more about, to our detriment.

A simple, early lesson when looking at the wind is to focus on gusts over average wind speed. Wind speed will tell you a lot (especially for a sailing boat) about how fast you'll get from A to B and will hint at the local sea state. Gusts are what you worry about, though. Strong gusts can make life difficult whether you're at anchor or underway.

The problem is that storm cells are, predictably, unpredictable. Weather forecasters can do an excellent job identifying the conditions that favour a storm developing. They just can't tell you precisely if a storm will hit.

In most advanced sailing-focused weather apps, there's a value called CAPE (Convective Available Potential Energy), which shows where the weather systems are volatile, and storms are likely to develop. What's not immediately apparent is that you can have both a high CAPE value (a strong possibility of a storm) and a low gust forecast. Storms tend to be highly localised and aren't reflected in the overall prediction. To put it another way, the general forecast could be for very little wind, except during that thirty minutes of mayhem when a storm cell sweeps through. It's just that no one knows when that thirty minutes will be or if it will even happen at all.

This is how we anchored off the island of Dhokos in a violent storm that swept south through the Saronic and into the Argolic Gulf. The forecast was for light winds, but the CAPE values were high. I'd selected the anchorage based on the potential for gusts but not the potential for storms.

It was another uneasy night where I spent it on anchor watch[2] until the winds passed, watching the 35+ knot gusts push us out to the edge of our swing circle where our anchor, properly set, held us without issues.

Beyond the storm, the night's drama came from the boat that anchored after us. There's an etiquette to anchoring. Essentially, it's first come, first served. We'd dropped our anchor in about ten metres of water and backed down with the wind into the SE corner of the anchorage in shallow water. A catamaran then came and dropped on the edge of the NW corner of our swing circle but didn't put out much chain.

As the storm swept in, the boats all spun around to the NW, and our chain dragged back, with the rear of *Matilda* moving towards the catamaran. When the catamaran dropped anchor, we'd been five or more boat lengths apart; now, we were only about two as we had more chain out than them and moved further on our swing.

Through the storm, I saw a flashlight flicking against the back window of our boat[3] and heard a cry, "*Matilda*, your anchor is dragging".

I went up, flashed a light to show that I had at least seen them and tried to communicate that we were fine; we weren't slipping; they'd just anchored a little close—a complex message in the wind[4].

Given we were confident that we weren't dragging, there wasn't much to do. They were now roughly two boat lengths behind us, but it may as well have been 500 metres (ca. 1/3 of a mile) for all the impact we could have on each other in the conditions.

Every ten minutes, they'd scream at us again until, eventually, the storm passed, and we all went to sleep. Other than swinging from one end of our anchor circle to the other, we hadn't dragged at all.

In the morning, the catamaran disappeared early, and another boat, a few boat lengths off to the side from us, called out.

---

2. Literally staying awake and watching the anchor to make sure nothing goes wrong and the boat doesn't drag.

3. This is a good way to get attention of a boat at anchor, flash a light over their portholes.

4. In hindsight, we should have tried to communicate on the VHF radio.

"Mate, we might have crossed chains here overnight. Just want you to know, we're about to pull up and go," said the skipper.

"Yeah, no worries, thanks for letting us know – I think we'll be okay; most of our chain should be out there," I said, pointing towards the SW corner of the anchorage.

The skipper looked at the departing catamaran, "What was his problem anyway? A lot of shouting last night."

"He thought we were dragging; he was worried we would hit his boat."

"Really? You guys looked fine to me. What an idiot."

Fortunately, in our small corner of the anchorage, we'd all escaped unscathed, but several other boats had pulled anchor and spent a few hours circling, waiting for conditions to settle. Not everyone had been as lucky or had set their anchors as well.

During the middle of the night, I'd heard a garbled conversation over the VHF radio with a sailboat, not in our anchorage, that ran aground.

"Coast Guard, this is sailing vessel X; we've lost our anchor and are now aground on Aegina. Seeking assistance."

"Sailing vessel X, this is Coast Guard. Is everyone safe?"

"Coast guard, this is sailing vessel X; yes, everyone is safely on shore. We're contacting you from a handheld."

"Sailing vessel X, this is the Coast Guard; clear the channel please; you're no longer a boat. Suggest you ring the police."

Once the boat had run aground, and everyone was safe, they were no longer the Coast Guard's problem. There were many others still at sea in the storm that needed their assistance.

Un-anticipated storms can be dangerous. Checking CAPE values to ensure we are aware of when and where storms might occur is now a big part of our weather planning. We can always tell a sailor who's been through a storm. When the CAPE values are up, they're heading with us back into a safe harbour on a sunny day to tuck away until the danger has passed while the charter boats all head out blissfully unaware.

The enemy of confidence is over-confidence, but it's also outside this comfort zone where growth occurs. Every so often, you have to push the envelope. We've grown the range of conditions we have experienced and are now willing to do more.

Thirteen

Planning

"The lovely thing about cruising is that planning usually turns out to be of little use." — Dom Degnon

Having successfully returned to the mainland, we decided to cross south to Poros. With good weather for the crossing, we were keen to show Hannah the best bits of travelling by boat and prove it wasn't all big waves and seasickness. At Poros, we could enjoy the atmosphere of the Greek village that stepped back up the hill, dressed in white and blue, with its iconic clock tower looming over the bay.

The journey went very smoothly, then we tied to the quay and toured the town briefly before sitting down at a cafe for lunch. At which point it promptly started to pour with rain, and a storm whipped through the anchorage. The chaos of the umbrellas at the cafe flapping while rain belted in, making everyone wet, caused me to run back to the boat to ensure everything was okay.

If there's a message in all this, it's that planning is of little use, yet you can't ignore making plans, either.

We were now only days from the end of our first season. Like others living aboard in the Med, we faced the dilemma of balancing the need to stay flexible and free with the reality of having to lock some things in and make them happen.

Facebook has several active yachting groups for cruisers and liveaboards. Some are globally focused, and others are strictly related to the Mediterranean or even just sailing in Greece.

We each have our version of a pirate fantasy. Buying a boat, then setting sail, free to explore the world and travel on a whim. These groups are full of people lamenting the fact that the dream has just run headlong into reality, crying into the ether:

"I can't check into Croatia; they won't let me stay without a sailing license! I sailed this boat from the USA; how can they say I can't sail my boat!"

"What do you mean I need a VHF license to get an MMSI[1]? And why can't I use that certificate I did with the RYA last year?"

"Call this freedom? What do you mean I have to commit to a marina in Türkiye for November now in April? What happens if I change my mind?"

Despite our desire to be free and to go as we please, life puts other requirements on us. Want to leave your boat safely on the hard somewhere and fly back home to Australia? You need to find a marina or a boatyard with space, make a commitment, pre-pay a deposit and then, yes, you better be there on time, ready for them to haul out. If not, you'll be stuck waiting because they are flat-out hauling and storing boats for the winter at that time of year. And you'll need to book it early because the marinas fill up with boats all wanting to do the same thing, or you won't find a place.

Our plan, put in place a few months earlier with our friends Markus and Isa, was to haul out at a boatyard on the north of Aegina. We'd set the date, somewhat arbitrarily, for the 1st of December. Now, with the date rapidly approaching, the weather wasn't cooperating.

From Poros, we took Hannah back to Aegina and then, two days before we were due to haul out, Markus called me.

"The weather is terrible. This strong north-westerly wind is horrible here in the harbour; a catamaran was damaged. You should call the boatyard and see if they can pull you out right now before it picks up again tonight," he said.

So we did. I immediately called the boatyard, and an hour later, we were out of the water. Beyond companionship, it's those moments that make relationships gold. Having someone else who cares and is looking out for you makes a big difference.

Poor Hannah! She'd left us to go and tour the Temple of Aphaia in the centre of Aegina, and she wasn't even able to complete that in peace without plans changing. She had to make her way to the boatyard to find us in disarray, *Matilda* up on the hard and us rushing about trying to tidy up to leave the boat. A far cry from the earlier plan of waving

---

1. An electronic serial number for boats. It's essential for AIS that lets you be seen by others.

goodbye to her on the ferry in the port then slowly preparing for our haul out two days later.

Without fail, the times we've been unhappiest onboard *Matilda* have been those where we have a deadline. The need to be somewhere at a specific time drives making choices that you would avoid in the ordinary course of things.

Our first season had just come to a close. *Matilda* was now safely on the hard, and we headed back to an apartment in Athens to wait out the winter, eager for season two to commence.

***

It may not be a written design constraint, but frankly, boats are built to test relationships. It's one thing to live together in a family home with multiple bedrooms, living rooms, etc. But it's entirely different on a boat, where you're within sight and sound of each other for the vast majority of the time.

Sometimes, living closely on a boat is intentional. Underway, you always want to know where the other person is. "I'm going below" is prudent information to share so that the person on the helm isn't worrying if they have a person overboard. Usually, though, that closeness is just a function of the limited space available in which to be.

Time apart was part of our daily existence in our previous corporate lives. We would go to work at different locations and in different cars. We'd travel to different cities and even different countries for days or weeks at a time. Now, on *Matilda*, some weeks pass by where we are never further apart than 10 metres (ca. 33 ft) for more than a few minutes.

Maybe one of us heads to the showers onshore or runs an errand to the shops, but quickly, we're back aboard in the main salon, sitting on the L-shaped couch only a metre or two apart. As I write this, I'm sitting at the table on my laptop while Karina is all of 1 metre (ca. 3.2 ft) away, watching TV. Ultimately, we spend most of our time on *Matilda* together, in sight and sound of each other.

At anchor or on a passage, this dynamic changes even more.

When you're tired, you're not always at your best. It's easy to be short with each other when you've had limited sleep over a series of days due to rough weather. Even at anchor or

in a marina, the water slapping on the hull or the clanging of halyards[2] on neigh-
bouring boats can keep you awake. You react in undesirable ways that you wouldn't
usually when well rested.

Now, take those frustrations, annoyances, and nitpicks that all couples will feel
together and limit the space you share to a boat—fourteen metres (ca. 46 ft) from
bow sprit to swim deck to find a private area. While we don't argue often, we're also
human, and it does happen. There's limited room to separate and "cool off", which
is even worse in the heat of summer, where the only place that's easy to stay during
the day is up on the flybridge.

We've learnt to be more tolerant and forgiving of each other. It's important to
listen, let each other vent and not be defensive when there's criticism. While neither
of us is perfect, sometimes it's just the heat and frustration with the weather that's
talking. A swim to cool down and saying "Sorry" afterwards goes a long way.

When you're on a boat, there is a new dynamic, too. Someone has to be the captain.

We've spoken with a lot of liveaboard couples, and navigating this relationship and
its changing hierarchy is one of the most challenging experiences to work through.
When things are going wrong, and a decision needs to be made, a boat is no place for
a democracy.

It's very evident when crossing borders and checking into another country. One
of the first questions on the crew list, the paperwork you need to provide, will be
some form of "Who is the captain?" No matter how much you want to explain that
responsibility on board is shared, as far as the authorities and your insurance are
concerned — some "one" is responsible for the boat.

For most of our 30+ years together, we've been co-decision makers. Yes, sometimes
one of us is more passionate about a project than the other or leads more in one part
of life, but it's seldom black and white. A boat is different.

We spoke a lot about this very early on. While it was clear that I'd be skipper
— given I was the one with both the appropriate qualifications and what little
experience we had — we needed to think through how it would work in practice.

We settled on an arrangement, which we've since found is quite common among
liveaboard couples. I'm the captain, but Karina is the admiral. In practice, for us, the way

---

2. Sailors will insist this is a rope to haul up the mainsail. I'm convinced its main use is to torture everyone
nearby with the incessant sound of the rope banging against a hollow aluminium mast.

this works is that Karina decides where we go. When it comes to how we get there, when we go, and what happens underway, I have control.

As admiral, Karina will decide (with some joint discussion) that we will go to Venice by May to meet with our daughter. I get to determine how we do that. What's the weather? When do we have to leave our winter berth to make that happen? Once I've identified several reasonable options, I'll put those to her for us to discuss and for her to choose one. When it comes to go or no-go, though, anything impacting the safety of the crew and the boat, that's on me.

This partnership works reasonably well, with each of us compromising and accepting that the other has the final say in their area of responsibility. It's easier said than done, especially as it's still inherently imbalanced. Day to day, there's more responsibility and decisions to be made concerning safety than there is about destinations. This imbalance can rub on us both in different ways.

I think the first time we were aware of this was at the end of the first season. Back in Athens and settling into our winter life without a boat, I was surprised at how tired I felt. For the first several days, I slept like the dead and didn't want to do anything apart from nest at home.

"What's wrong?" Karina asked.

"Nothing, I'm just exhausted."

Months of feeling the need to constantly be alert, listening for every unusual sound, worried about the weather, the wind, and the swell had worn me down in a way I'd not realised or accounted for. As a society, we're much more cognisant these days about mental load, the idea that you're carrying consideration for something that the other person is unconcerned about. When it comes to the galley, perhaps unsurprisingly, this is Karina. I go through life without worrying too much about where my next meal is coming from.

As captain, I'd been carrying the responsibility of safety on board *Matilda*. Of course, we shared this during the day, but at night, when we'd tuck into bed on anchor, Karina slept better while I started at every slight noise.

In many ways, it's a reassuring vote of confidence. A relaxed crew is a crew that trusts you. What I needed to learn was to trust the boat. I've become more relaxed as I gain experience with the gear we use and the range of conditions it works in. I sleep much better, but I'm still the first to startle awake during a gust to ensure everything is fine.

With *Matilda* safe in the boatyard and Karina and I back in an apartment in Athens, I slept deeper than I had in months. Some habits were hard to shake like checking the wind updates every few hours, something that's irrelevant living in a city. With every storm system that passed us by, it was further validation that we'd made the right call to step off *Matilda* during the winter months.

As each day passed, helping us to unwind, it also reinforced the value of something we'd been thinking about since a conversation with Markus and Isa when we first met them.

During August, Greece can be challenging — it's the most popular time for charters, the weather is often sweltering, and all the anchorages and beaches are crowded. We were lamenting this experience when we first met them, when Isa said, "That's why we always go home to Bavaria in August."

It was a revelation: why not go "the opposite direction" to everyone else, leaving Greece when it's too hot and crowded? Now, back in our apartment and enjoying the break from being on the water while also yearning to get back out there, we saw the value in what they said.

Sure, we are full-time cruisers, but if we lived in a house, we'd also take holidays and travel too. Being a liveaboard doesn't mean you have to spend every waking moment on your boat. One of the first things we did while waiting for winter to end was plan where we'd be in August and how we might take a break from *Matilda* too.

***

Once you're in the cruising community, it never really leaves you, even when you're back on land. Along with the friendships, the desire to tell tall tales and a lust for adventure became a part of the everyday. While we continued waiting for work to be completed on *Matilda*, I was browsing Facebook groups.

In one, an Australian sailor, Brad, was asking for someone to help him out with a video tour of a boat in Greece that he wanted to buy. He was in the Caribbean, having sold his current boat, and wanted to buy a used boat in Greece to explore new cruising grounds.

Before boarding the plane, however, he needed slightly more assurance that the used charter boat he was interested in purchasing was in decent condition. The idea of hopping back on a boat, any boat, was very appealing, and with plenty of time available, I offered to go and inspect it for him. The plan was for me to poke and prod everything Brad wanted to see in more detail while on video instead of him relying on the broker, who may not be trustworthy. The tour was a success, and we continued to chat afterwards when it was complete.

When I asked him how he got to the Caribbean, he replied, "Oh, I bought a boat in Spain a couple of years ago. I had no idea how to sail, so I taught myself on YouTube and then a couple of weeks after that... I just sailed it across the Atlantic."

HE. JUST. SAILED. IT. ACROSS. THE. ATLANTIC. With no experience beyond two weeks on his boat and a few YouTube videos.

If experience and planning aren't necessary, then plain old dumb luck will take you a long way. If it's any consolation, Brad did say afterwards that knowing what he knows now, he wouldn't do it that way again. Don't try that one at home, kids.

In some ways, he'd learnt the lessons of that adventure. His inspection of this new boat was meticulous; the questions and knowledge of the systems and potential problems hard won by owning a boat that had manifested all the things that could go wrong. Planning had now come to the forefront. Still, in the absence of good planning and experience, confidence and a willingness to give it a go will take you much further than it has any right to.

***

While planning around deadlines can be frustrating and difficult, planning how to handle emergencies is essential. Fortunately, there's a lot of time on a boat. Cruising from A to B can leave plenty of time for a conversation or two with the crew to discuss what might happen if a condition eventuates.

As we continued to wait for *Matilda* to have her winter work completed and the weather to improve so we could launch her for the season, I had the opportunity to deliver a sailing boat around the Peloponnese. I jumped at it! While it would be a challenge, I felt well-prepared for it. With my experience now on *Matilda*, the chance to get back on a sailboat and cruise in Greece was welcome.

There was just one issue. I also needed to bring the crew.

No worries, I had a phone full of contacts for people we'd met cruising and travelling Greece. By the end of the day, Mark and Elizabeth, whom we'd met in Porto Cheli and Peter, a Facebook contact I'd yet to meet in person, had all agreed to hop aboard. We'd set off in four days to help deliver a Jeanneau 42 sailboat from Athens to the island of Kefalonia, taking the long way south around the base of the Peloponnese Peninsula.

Covering this many nautical miles in a short time meant plenty of time while underway to play "what-if" with the crew. This is a great way to increase your confidence and experience and be prepared for an emergency.

As we set sail from the island of Spetses, heading to Monemvasia and beyond, I mused, "What would we do if the electronics failed?"

"We have paper charts onboard..." said Elizabeth.

Mark chimed in with, "...and we can navigate by sight everywhere around here. We've all sailed here before, so we have the local knowledge needed to get to port okay."

"But, we'd want to work out what caused the failure first, though," added Elizabeth.

No more than thirty minutes after this conversation, the electronics on the boat failed. The batteries were not charging while the motor was underway, and anything electrical on the boat had just switched off. The best guess was that the alternator had failed. Fortunately, the engine was still running.

And yes, we knew where we were, had local knowledge and could easily reach our destination, but after consulting the charter operator, we turned back to a nearby port behind us. It made the most sense to meet their mechanic there so they could replace the alternator.

Two nights after this, we discussed anchoring during a storm. "So what do you do when the wind picks up and the anchor starts dragging?" asked Elizabeth.

"The first step is to turn on the motor and steer into the wind to take pressure off the chain," was my answer. Not something I'd ever done before, but endless YouTube videos seemed to suggest this would be the right course of action.

You guessed it. Later that night, a storm swept our anchorage, and several boats in our fleet lost their hold. They hauled in their anchors and spent an eventful half hour finding new positions while the wind gusted around the bay, making things difficult.

The bay was very sheltered from the south, and it initially seemed we'd have good shelter there. We hadn't accounted for the sweeping curve of the cliffs at the northern end of the bay. They caught the wind, curling the gusts around and onto the boats, all anchored in the supposedly sheltered corner. Instead of from the south, in that bay, we experienced the winds from the north.

Luckily, our boat held okay. We'd arrived early enough in the daylight to pick a prime position and had ensured our anchor was well set. Just after 11 pm, as the winds started to gust up above 40 knots, we ran the motor, idling forward in gear into the wind to protect the hold. The storm was fierce but relatively brief. We held an anchor watch until around 1 am, then collapsed into bed.

A more superstitious crew would have given up on talking about disasters at this point. Not us! Ever willing to learn and challenge ourselves on the last day of the delivery, we turned our what-ifs to consider a complete engine failure.

As we rounded the point south of the island of Kefalonia, just off the coast from the town of Skala, the wind that had pushed us northwards at almost 9 knots died away. We put the sails away and decided to cruise the last ten nautical miles using the motor to complete the delivery.

As the crew headed downstairs to make lunch, I fired up the motor and set course for the port of Sami. Not two minutes later, the engine, which hadn't skipped a beat the last 400 nautical miles, started sounding an alarm. It was overheating.

I stopped it, and then we put the sails back out to regain some control in the light winds. Although we were in no immediate danger, drifting idly without power a mile offshore seemed a poor choice. With some headway being made, a mere 1.5 knots over the ground against the current pushing south, we started the diagnosis process.

While we weren't sure, but it seemed most likely that the impellor had failed. Without it, no water was discharging over the side when the engine ran, and without water being sucked through the motor to cool it, it was overheating. In an emergency, we could use the engine for a minute or so, but more than that could cause severe damage.

As we'd discussed earlier in the day, we then got to test our sailing skills to the extreme. Firstly, dealing with a current against us and very light wind, we had to sail for almost 3 hours to get up and around the point only a few nautical miles away. Once cleared, we turned towards the nearest safe port, Poros[3].

Then, the wind gusted up behind us now that we were clear of the blocking effect of the island's eastern edge, and we raced the last few miles. We furled the mainsail and entered the port using the genoa only. This lets you quickly lose momentum as you can "let the genoa go", causing it to flap madly. If you time it right, you can coast right to the dock. We came close to the dock but fell short; a quick burst of the motor, now cool again after being off for the last few hours, saw us safely tied up ashore.

---

3. At times in Greece, names are repetitive! This was Poros, Kefalonia, not the island of Poros.

A mechanic met us and quickly replaced the impellor, which was missing most of its fins. When we tested the motor with a new impellor, water ran through the engine and spat out bits of mangled rubber fins and melted white plastic. We never found out what caused the failure, but the immediate problem was repaired, and in short order, we were clear to go again.

I asked the crew what we should do. We all had flights the following day, and after a week at sea, we were all keen to wrap the delivery up and return home. While leaving the boat in Poros was an option, we were determined to say, "We did it", and complete the delivery to Sami. So, we set off back to sea to motor the hour and a bit up the coast to our final destination.

About five minutes out of port, as I checked over the engine again, I saw water spilling into the bilge under the engine mounts.

I came back to deliver the news to the crew. "Ahh, so, it looks like we're taking on water..."

The plastic mixer elbow, which combines the cooling water and the exhaust before expelling it, had melted when the engine overheated[4]. Now, whenever the engine ran, it leaked water into the boat. It was time to give up. We flipped the manual bilge pumps on, turned back to Poros, docked the boat again, and, at that point, declared it delivered. The mechanic arrived and confirmed the problem with the elbow – it would take a couple of days to get a spare from Athens, but it was no longer our issue.

While I was always confident we'd be successful — I also knew it would be a test of my growing abilities. I didn't realise how much! Managing a failing sailboat on its first trip of the season, some 400 nautical miles around the Peloponnese in poor weather without any issues, was a challenge. But, as a crew, we'd put significant effort into planning along the way. We knew our roles and rose to meet and overcome each challenge. Despite the difficulties, we were proud of what we'd achieved and finished with a healthy respect for the sorts of things that could go wrong and a confidence we could handle them when they inevitably did.

***

---

4. With hindsight, this is probably the white plastic that was spat out when we restarted the engine.

Despite the drama of that journey around the Peloponnese, it was in most ways that it matters, actually relatively undramatic. The boat went out, and some things went wrong; they were managed, and the boat got (almost) to where it needed to be. To sail a boat requires a degree of risk. We all have our own tolerance for the right level of risk we're willing to take. The challenge is to balance it with our appetite for adventure.

Some people never do. We met one couple who had set off to pursue the dream, and after multiple setbacks in buying a boat, they'd eventually found one which they purchased sight unseen. When they arrived on board, they quickly put it up for sale again within a few weeks without leaving the harbour. The realities of the compressed space, even on a large catamaran, was something they quickly decided they weren't willing to handle if they wanted to stay married.

The wife, in particular, was nervous and quickly moved into an apartment ashore. It was clear she would never stay on the boat at anchor when she was terrified of every little movement while tied up and sheltered in a marina. I maintain this was the right decision for them. I think it's smart to step back when you realise it's not for you. It turns out the level of risk they were comfortable tolerating together was almost zero, and they'd never go anywhere by boat.

For others, there's no risk too big. Chasing Bubbles is a documentary (available on Netflix at the time of writing) that tells the story of Alex Rust. He decided to toss in his life as a stockbroker and chase the dream of sailing the world. For Alex, it seemed there was no risk too huge. He bought a boat without any sailing knowledge, trying to learn to sail by reading "Sailing for Dummies" while out on the water. With no experience or training, he set off for the Bahamas. He spent his first season working his way south before eventually crossing through the Panama Canal and circumnavigating the world over the next five years.

It's something we would never do. According to our friends, we're generally perceived as brave adventurers. Still, the reality is our tolerance for risk and true adventure is pretty low, with Karina's generally speaking lower than mine. Certainly, our tolerance for the discomfort accompanying that throw-yourself-into-it-and-just-do-it approach no longer matches our lifestyle. But, I do wonder if, back in the day, when we first met, we'd have benefited from a little less dreaming and a bit more doing.

The reality is that there are plenty of ways of cruising the world, and you can manage risk pretty well. I will probably never convince Karina to circumnavigate with me, do an Atlantic crossing, or even round the Peloponnese in a sailboat! But there are plenty of cruising grounds that she is keen to enjoy. You can cruise and explore without spending weeks at sea if that's what you want.

Most likely, the most significant thing people fear (after getting seasick) is, "What happens if the boat sinks?"

While boats do sink, it's an improbable occurrence. When you're coastal cruising like we are in the Mediterranean, it's also rarely fatal, even if it does occur.

Let's take Greece, for example. It has roughly 2,650 charter yachts (second only to Croatia, which has nearly 4,500), and Alimos harbour in Athens is the world's biggest charter base, with around 8% of the global yacht charter fleet located there. A back-of-the-envelope calculation suggests that in Greece, there are about 37,000 week-long journeys by charter boat in summer! Most of these are undertaken by skippers with little more than a few weeks of actual training and maybe a previous charter if they are lucky.

Very few of these charter trips end with anything more concerning than a few scrapes and bumps or perhaps damage to a keel or rudder if they run aground. Occasionally, the damage will be severe enough that the charter boat is written off.

It's big news when a charter boat sinks; everyone talks about it, analyses it, and wonders what went wrong. I know a handful in Greece over the last couple of years. I've heard of one boat in big seas that failed to shut its forward hatch, swamping it and causing the crew to seek rescue.

The most serious was a lightning strike. A catamaran that, by all accounts, should never have decided to sail when they did was at the end of their charter and returning to Alimos. The lightning strike killed both engines in the storm, and big waves smashed the boat onto the rocks outside the marina. All the crew escaped to shore successfully, although the catamaran was written off as a complete wreck.

There was the boat I already mentioned, which ran aground during the storm and where they had the conversation with the Coast Guard, "We can't help you; you're no longer a boat." I don't know the outcome here, but probably the boat was re-floated shortly afterwards, then taken to a shipyard for checks and repairs if needed.

It's fair to say that boating is generally very safe for the type of cruising common here in the Mediterranean. You're more likely to get injured by things within your control (collision with another boat, for example), and basic good seamanship practices can avoid that. While the weather in the Mediterranean is occasionally volatile, and massive storms can periodically sweep in and damage boats at anchor, the risks to life and limb are low, especially on a well-prepared boat.

Of course, when you talk about blue-water ocean cruising, the boat being away from shore for long periods, the levels of risk do increase. Incidents that in the Mediterranean might be a dangerous inconvenience can become life-threatening when you're days away from assistance. But thousands of people a year cruise safely, crossing the Atlantic and exploring the Pacific with little more than a bad sunburn. Preparation is key.

Nothing is entirely risk-free, but a fear of danger shouldn't hold you back. Well-managed liveaboard cruising is not an extreme sport, especially when hopping from port to port and not racing across the Atlantic. It's easy to manage risk to a level you're comfortable with, and the key to that is good planning.

***

With the boat delivery completed, Karina and I returned to Aegina, where it was time to launch *Matilda* back into the water. Like all good plans involving boats, things weren't quite going the way we'd envisaged. One of our major upgrades was adding an air conditioner. Still, despite being scheduled for completion in early March, it had continued to be delayed due to parts being on backorder.

By late March, we'd had enough. We were ready to start cruising again and wanted the boat back in the water. The key to managing any good plan is to be flexible. Part of the urgency was that we knew we'd have to leave for a month in May to head to the USA. We decided to launch *Matilda* immediately, cruise for a few weeks, and then haul her out again. This way, we could explore for a few weeks and then, hopefully, the missing parts would arrive, and the work could be completed while we were travelling.

In almost as much of a rush as she came out of the water, *Matilda* was back afloat, and season two had commenced.

Fourteen

Relationships

"Two captains sink a ship." — Turkish Proverb

As we started our second season, we were excited to share *Matilda* with friends again. In our first season, we had started and finished so late that we didn't always get the best of the weather. The true Greek summer experience of sitting out in tavernas, swimming in warm seas and blue skies, had passed us by.

But before we could start welcoming guests aboard, we had to relearn how to cruise *Matilda* ourselves. A winter on the shore meant numerous little things about the systems on board had been forgotten. This could be as trivial as remembering to start the shower sump before showering; other times, it was making sure the drain plug was re-inserted into the tender before launching it [1]!

It quickly came back, and we didn't embarrass ourselves in those first few weeks, but it was also clear that our dynamic had changed. Whereas before, Karina would look to me for instructions on most things, now she'd gained confidence and ability after our first season and had opinions of her own. Like everything new, navigating this new way of operating took some time.

While Karina's one of the first to admit she didn't see her life becoming a full-time live-aboard, once the decision was made, she embraced it. She always wants to be competent on the boat. To learn more and become more skilled. The challenge we were now facing

---

1. Alternatively, you can watch your tender pretend to be a submarine.

was how this played out in moments where things were, if not a full-blown emergency, perhaps getting a bit hairy.

Whenever you're on the helm, you're often thinking about several things at once, and it's not uncommon to issue one instruction; then, as a situation evolves, notice something else that needs attention. Or maybe it's just as things change quickly, you see something requiring more urgent attention. Early on, Karina would just do as instructed, but now, she wanted to understand the "why". She started to get frustrated when it appeared I was changing my mind.

Which, to be fair, is precisely what happens occasionally! As the situation unfolds when we pull into a harbour, I've definitely called out, "Let's switch the fenders from port to starboard."

"But you said you were coming alongside on port!" Karina replies exasperatedly.

"I changed my mind!"

There are lessons here for both of us. At one level, you could say Karina needs to roll with things, tackle the task at hand and follow up afterwards when things have become unclear. But that ignores the fact that I need to explain better why I want to do something and, even more importantly, learn that sometimes, there's no need to vary the plan.

It's taken me time to understand that often, there's no need to be 100% "by the book". I tend to be a reasonably studious sailor. I like to know the rules and regulations, and I like to know the right way to do something. At least, if not the right way, I want to have a well-reasoned explanation as to why I'm doing it differently.

Why does this matter? Why not just do the most correct thing all the time?

Take the simple example of docking alongside. Of course, in Greece, nothing is ever that simple! Pulling into a port, there can be all sorts of hidden obstacles or other boats placed seemingly at random. As much as we try to pre-plan what we do, these factors introduce some variables at the point we're coming to the dock.

Perhaps I called to set up the fenders so we could come alongside on the starboard side. Now that we're in the port, there might be more room than I thought. Going through my mind is the thought that if we spin the boat, I can reverse alongside (on our port side) so we can leave more easily the next day. Maybe the wind is different inside the port. Whatever it is, at that moment, several little things play together and can lead to a slightly more optimal decision.

I'm learning that changing the plan part way isn't worth the confusion it inevitably creates unless it's a significant improvement. It's far simpler to have a straightforward course of action and follow through than it is to chop and change just because, currently, one approach is incrementally better than the other. Of course, we change the plan if something impacts the safety of the boat or crew. But we both execute more effectively when we don't change unnecessarily.

The more we cruise together, the better we understand each other, our moods, the boat, and the conditions. Every so often, it's just knowing that when I call "port", you need to check because I clearly meant to call "starboard!" Forgiveness is an important skill. If you search "Forgive me for what I said while docking the boat," endless T-shirts and coffee mugs are dedicated to this simple phrase. It's not the going that's the problem; it's the stopping.

Stress is usually an avoidable issue. Docking, like most things on a boat, is best done calmly and predictably. The need to yell at each other is a failure in planning and training. Planning, because as captain, I should ensure that there is a plan A, B and C. Even more importantly, I need to ensure these are clearly explained beforehand. Training, because we both need to understand how to communicate with each other effectively and that we have the skills to execute.

Where possible, we use hand signals to indicate what we want the other to do, but eventually, a situation will arise where we need to talk. Another valuable realisation is that speaking loudly is not necessarily shouting. You need to project your voice with the wind and other conditions in a port.

There's a subtle difference between projection and shouting. One is clearly and loudly, relaying information concisely. The other is a frustrated captain, and if they are sufficiently self-aware, regretting their lack of planning and communication. Some couples use walkie-talkie style headsets — they have a common nickname in the liveaboard community, "Marriage Savers".

Planning is always essential, but equally valuable is debriefing afterwards. Regardless of how things went, we constantly do a debrief together on what went well and what we could improve. The debrief can be as simple as a high five celebrating a good job — there is nothing more to say.

But when things haven't gone smoothly, it's a great time to put the captain's hat aside and listen. With the task at hand complete and the boat safe, we can discuss options, what went well and what could have been done differently. Karina's developed a lot of experience and has countless great ideas, too. While in the moment, it's best to act with one voice; if you want to continue having a successful relationship on board, you must also put your ego aside and listen to good suggestions.

When you're short-handed, it's critical to ensure that you share the skills and knowledge and are both capable in all roles. Too often, we see skippers who fail to let their partner "have a go". Sometimes, despite the encouragement, it's the partners who are too scared to try to learn to manoeuvre the boat at close quarters.

A typical pattern on less experienced boats is that the men on board hog the wheel. With more experienced boats, you'll regularly see the women on board at the helm. It makes a lot of sense. I'm stronger than Karina, and when going stern-to, the lines, especially lazy lines[2], take physical strength to set correctly. Karina is very capable on the helm, so when docking, she's typically there while I secure the lines. It also means that we're both cross-skilled in both roles. Just because I can handle the lines more effectively doesn't mean she can't do it if needed.

If there's ever an emergency on board where I'm unable to assist, Karina is equally capable of safely piloting us where we need to go and docking the boat. A quiet confidence in each other's skills is much better than shouting.

Ultimately, despite the challenges along the way, there's nothing more satisfying as a couple than realising you're in this together. There's a joy in making it work for you both that's respectful but also practical to the needs of the boat.

We worked through this changing dynamic and now make a better team because of it, with a sound foundation for tackling the bigger challenges to come.

***

We explored more of the Saronic Gulf, then hauled out again for a month to travel to the US. Towards the end of May, finally, we were set off again for real. Our goal was to head around the bottom of Greece (the Peloponnese), then up through the Ionian Sea that borders its western edge. From there, Albania and eventually Montenegro and Croatia.

Fortunately, the weather in late May was much better behaved for our trip around the Peloponnese than my earlier journey with Mark and Elizabeth. The various storms and

---

2. Instead of dropping your anchor, lazy lines are already fastened to the seabed. You tie them to the bow of your boat. Despite the fact they are supposedly easier, hence lazy, they always seem more work than just dropping anchor!

challenges I'd faced with them on that trip never eventuated, and we quickly made our way around the south of Greece into the Ionian.

***

Having made it to the Ionian, we met with friends from Athens. We headed from the mainland of Katokalo, near the ancient site of the Olympic Games, towards Zakynthos and a turtle sanctuary.

While guests are one of the delights of life aboard, like fish, they can start to go off after a few days, too. We love having guests and always encourage them to come and stay, but we're also happy when they go. With such a small space, you inevitably start to trip over each other and get in each other's way.

So much of life on a boat is structured. Things are done in a specific way for particular reasons that are very different from on land. A typical example on most boats is how water is managed. Although we have a watermaker on board, one of our favourite items, which means we can create drinking water in most locations, water is still a precious commodity. It's a finite resource, which means we wash dishes in a specific way to reduce our water usage as much as possible.

For example, we never stack dirty plates. Why? Because then the bottom stays clean, and you only have to wash the dirty side!

Guests always offer to help, which is appreciated, but when they collect and stack the plates and then wash the dishes as they are used to, where water is an endless commodity from the tap, their water usage always seems excessive. With each groan of the water pump, we cringe, envisaging wasted water pouring into the sea. It seems trivial to tell someone trying to help, "Here's how you wash the dishes", so I end up biting my tongue or telling them, "Not to worry, I'll just do it myself".

Those guests with experience on the sea or even on board *Matilda* already are great. They typically have the basic skills, like how to tie a few knots, handle the lines, etc. Even more importantly, those with a lot of experience on boats understand the importance of sitting down and shutting up.

On one occasion, with a particularly inquisitive guest who in all other respects was an absolute pleasure to be with, we've had to say, "Now's not the time for questions; just hold them until we're docked." In fact, now, we tell this to all our guests when we think we will be in a stressful moment.

It's frustrating enough dealing with a challenging docking experience without worrying about someone wandering around on deck inspecting everything you do and asking, "Why did you do that?"

Our best guests are those who are liveaboard sailors themselves. They are always happy to sit back, relax and let someone else do the work for a change! They will lend a competent hand if asked but won't get in the way otherwise. It's something I also try to be conscious of on other people's boats myself. We all dread the friendly skipper who always has a different way of doing something. "Oh, interesting – you know, I'd do it this way instead."

Ultimately, as long as the boat is being operated safely, we try to sit down and shut up as guests. We'll offer to help up front, but beyond that, we wait to be told. You know that liveaboard couples have their own way of doing things, and they are entirely capable of handling their boat by themselves.

As we always tell our guests when they board, "Please let us know if you want to help; we're happy to teach you but don't feel you have to. We handle *Matilda* ourselves all the time; you won't offend us if you sit back and enjoy the ride."

One of the people we were most nervous about having on board was Iain, a well-experienced powerboat skipper. A retired police sergeant, he'd been a member of the water police, operated high-speed RIBs, owned several boats and was an RYA Examiner. Despite his relaxed attitude, we couldn't help but feel like we had a driving instructor on board. Thankfully, he didn't care, just happy to be out on the water enjoying the ride without doing any of the work.

Docked up again after a day exploring local bays, we asked for his feedback. "Anything we should have done better?"

"Maybe served a few more beers to the guests? It all looked great to me. Boat got out, boat got back. Didn't hit anything, what more do you want?" he replied laconically.

While there were undoubtedly a few things that Iain could have critiqued and commented on, he also knew something that many "experienced" armchair sailors forget. While there are endless "best ways" of doing something, ultimately, the goal is to make it out and back again safely and for the guests to enjoy themselves. Iain's welcome aboard *Matilda* any time. He knows the most important rule. That boating, for all its challenges, is meant to be fun.

***

Guests also put other strains on your relationships. Intimacy, a.k.a. sex, generally has to take a back seat. With around 7 metres (ca. 23 ft) between the door to the guest cabin and the door to the main cabin, discretion is key. Not a lot goes unheard in a small space, especially when we encourage everyone to keep their door open in the heat of summer to promote airflow throughout the boat.

This is all to be expected. What came as a surprise was some other restrictions on intimacy when you're at a town quay.

It varies from boat to boat, but in *Matilda*, we have a stern main cabin with the guest cabin up in the bow. There are various pros and cons of sleeping in a stern vs. bow cabin, but one of the significant advantages of the stern cabin is that boats are generally wider at the rear. You'll have a bigger bed at the stern.

In Greece, where stern-to-mooring is very common on a town quay, that also means that you might be sleeping only a few metres away from a taverna, your head only 2 metres (ca. 6.5 ft) away from the dock. Depending on the layout of the port, you might even have tables on the dock beside you, with people eating and drinking a few metres away.

Many a sailor in Greece has bemoaned the sound of a taverna playing Greek music loudly until 2 am while they desperately try to sleep. While boats are waterproof, they aren't great at soundproofing. With the summer heat and the need to create airflow, hatches and windows in the cabin are often left ajar—a necessary tradeoff between listening to loud music or sweltering in bed overnight.

Come the next morning, I'm sure we are not the only liveaboard couple that's been 'interrupted' by the hacking post-cigarette cough of an elderly Greek man strolling along the town quay. Or worse, sitting on the bench just a few metres from the open window enjoying his early morning coffee. I'll leave it to your imagination, but at that point, if you can hear them so clearly, they can hear you, too.

***

As we continued through the season, another challenge we faced was managing relationships with family and friends ashore. This is something that's not just specific to sailors. Whether it's moving countries, changing jobs or leaving your long-term friends in their hometown to travel full-time, significant changes in your life alter your experiences and perspectives. But it makes navigating existing relationships harder when you no longer share the same framework for connecting.

For sailors, the demographic of liveaboards in the Med is predominantly retired couples, typically parents who have grown children. While your kids might be excited to come and spend time with you, it's no guarantee. For some people, our daughter included, the idea of being at sea is terrifying — not something she wants to do as a holiday!

Timing and cost are also an issue. In most cases, you will be sailing in warmer climates – the Mediterranean, Caribbean, or South Pacific. These are all destinations that, when you're from the UK, USA, Canada, Australia or NZ, are remote and difficult to get to in varying degrees. We've had to accept that as much as our friends and family might love to join us aboard, it's just not as practical for them as it is for us, who have time on our hands.

Our daughter reminded us of this in no uncertain terms when we tried to convince her to join us for a quick getaway to a city in Europe over winter. Even with the offer of paying her airfare from Edinburgh, she quickly pointed out, "I think you've forgotten what it's like to work. I can't just run off whenever. I actually have a job! Besides, I have to save my leave if I'm going to come visit over the summer."

When speaking with old friends and work colleagues, it can be hard to relate to their problems and for them to connect to ours. I no longer care about who said what to whom at work. They don't appreciate why I'm so excited about the local chandlery stocking precisely the right model of macerator pump so I can repair my head without delay!

As a liveaboard, your boat becomes all-consuming. Our conversations tend towards what broke, what needs fixing, where we've been and where we're going. But, for friends and family back onshore, they can't always appreciate why you're excited and, perhaps, are rightly fed up with the otherwise idyllic life you appear to live while they are stuck at work.

From the first season, when everyone, including us, was just excited that we had finally found a boat, things started to feel somewhat more mundane in the second season. While there was still plenty of adventure, the milestones were now (thankfully) often just the simple joy of an anchorage to ourselves, something that is hard for non-sailors to appreciate. It's also tough for those still working. No one wants to hear your tales of swimming in the crystal waters of the warm Mediterranean Sea while it's winter where they are.

"Don't you get bored?" They ask.

We don't.

All we can do is keep trying to find that connection, a destination they are equally excited about exploring to share with us, too, and see why this life is so compelling. We love sharing the joy of what we have, and being able to do so with others is one of the best parts of this experience.

***

We continued north to Kefalonia and then across to the island of Ithaca, the mythical home of Odysseus. Sitting back on the flybridge one afternoon while watching the boats come and go, a charter boat snagged our chain.

We started our engines, put the boat into gear against the stern lines, and then loosened the chain to allow them to lift and unhook it. No matter how much we tried to explain what they needed to do from our boat, they weren't listening. Each one was yelling at the other, all throwing out ideas, but no one was willing to actually do anything. One of them even offered up what was a pretty good solution, but the others shouted them down.

Karina asked me, "Do you think they need help?"

"Should I go over? I don't want to interfere."

"Sure, but you know how to help them get free, right?"

She was right. It was clear they wouldn't resolve this without some outside help.

I called out, "Captain, would you like some advice?"

The obvious issue seemed to me that, while on paper at least, there must be someone designated skipper, in practice, they had no authority over the rest of the crew. I never figured out who was in charge, but after some discussion, one of the younger men called out, "Yes, please!"

"If you like, I'm happy to come to the boat and help you get unstuck. But on one condition — I know how to do it, but you need to listen to me. If you would rather not listen, that's fine; I'll stay out of the way here. Your choice."

"You sure that's the right thing? You sound like a bit of an arsehole," Karina said quietly.

I knew it, but it was also clear that they needed some leadership. It would be easier for them to accept the advice of an outsider, but if they weren't happy to do that, I'd just be adding more noise to the problem.

There was a group conversation, and then one of the ladies on board yelled back, "That's great; we'd love you to come and help us out."

I swam over to their boat. "OK, so first things first, everyone is safe, you're not in any danger here, let's get this figured out. I saw you trying to pull up the anchor. Why did you stop?"

"Well, the windlass is making weird noises, and I was worried we would get stuck," answered another of the crew.

"OK, well, you're already stuck; let's see where we are at."

We tried the windlass again. The issue was that it was too underpowered to lift the chain and anchor, plus the added weight of our chain. The gypsy was also clearly worn, and it started slipping.

"Oh, it's been doing that a lot. The charter company says they'll get someone out to take a look," said the woman who had asked me to come aboard.

The windlass wouldn't cut it, so we briefly tried manually pulling the chain up. It was quickly apparent this was too dangerous. The weight of our chain and the anchor meant the chain quickly slipped back into the water, with the danger that fingers might get trapped. We needed an alternative solution.

"Let's tie a rope to the chain, run it back to the winch[3] in the cockpit, and we'll use that to pull it up," I instructed.

Within a few minutes, we had a rope running from the chain, tied with a rolling hitch and the rest back in the cockpit. With a few wraps around the winch, we were able to start winding it in. The chain and anchor started to come up, and we flaked the chain back into the locker.

Karina monitored our chain and let more out as required, allowing us to bring their anchor to deck level, visibly hooked onto our chain. We tried briefly to free it by passing a rope underneath, and then I looked up and saw Karina standing at the bow of *Matilda* with our chain release hook ready to go. One of the crew rushed over to collect it, and then I showed them how to catch the chain with the hook, tie the end off on a deck cleat and then drop their anchor to release it. Our chain dropped clear, finally free of their anchor. Pulling their anchor up again, they were now free, too.

"OK, that's it! You guys are good to go!" I told them.

"I told you we should have used a rope on the chain!" Exclaimed the woman who had invited me aboard to the rest of the crew.

---

3. It's a boat, it doesn't have to make sense. It's a windlass when it's a winch for chains, but it's a winch when it's for ropes. Unless the anchor rode is rope, then it's still a windlass. Got it?

She seemed more experienced than the others and was rightly exasperated that they'd been close to the solution. An inability to listen and act together had paralysed them. Although I'd helped, most of the assistance was in breaking the deadlock between the crew members and just choosing a course of action.

With their anchor now onboard, a quick test showed that the windlass would work when not hooked to our chain.

"What do we do if the windlass still isn't working?" Asked the maybe-but-not-quite-sure-if-they-were skipper.

I explained the process of flaking out the chain onto the deck and then throwing the anchor overboard manually in case they needed to do that if the windlass jammed.

"Better off heading to Sami over there," I pointed. "Tell them you have a problem and need to tie alongside while you get the charter company out. Anyway, at least if you get stuck, you know what to do now."

A bottle of wine under my arm as a thank you, it was back to *Matilda*, where Karina had already tightened our chain again. Everything worked exactly as it should on our end, and we were secure again.

The next day, I received a message from that same boat, again thanking us for the assistance and sharing that the charter company had repaired the windlass. They were underway to continue their holiday.

Boats require technical skill to operate, but the people skills are equally important. As skipper, you have to have the confidence to act. Boats aren't democracies; having a chain of command and acting and exercising it is critical. But you also have to be able to listen to each other and work as a team too.

The crew on the stuck boat came close to solving the problem themselves on several occasions. But the lack of anyone stepping up to make a call and a reluctance to try a few possible solutions left them floundering when they should have been able to free themselves.

If there's a line that separates a more experienced cruiser from the pure novice, I think it's understanding that a successful boat is all about relationships. Managing yourselves, your friends, and your interactions with others outside the boat. It all plays a part. It's that ability to interact, listen and act together in concert that lets you overcome adversity.

That feeling of experience is gained gradually, creeping up on you over time. Some days, you feel that together, you can achieve anything. The next, you've forgotten how to turn on the radio because you just spent six weeks away from the boat. Perhaps, as Martin, the round-the-world sailor we met in Milos, might say, there's nothing special to it at all. It's just stubbornness and confidence you'll figure it out.

We were proud of how we'd managed to help; for that moment, we felt that we'd levelled up together. We became sailors who had seen a thing or two and could confidently help others in a pinch.

Fifteen

Joy

"Believe me, my young friend, there is nothing – absolutely nothing – half so much worth doing as simply messing about in boats." — Kenneth Graham

S kippering a boat is all about personal responsibility. Things can and will go wrong. A boat on the water is a dynamic environment. Even if the disaster wasn't your fault, you have to act and move forward, dealing with it as best you can.

After the high of freeing the boat with the failing windlass, we'd chosen to stay in the same bay, although we moved location to the far end after a second boat lifted our anchor again! The anchorage was picturesque; we had time to spare, and our friends, Kerry and Keven, had anchored stern-to next to us. That evening, we enjoyed a drink together on *Matilda*, swapping stories and indulging in some harbour cinema.

There are, broadly speaking, two sorts of charterers. One is individuals with varying degrees of experience chartering a boat and cruising around. Like the group we'd just assisted. Personally, I have a lot of time for these people. We, too, know what it's like to be overwhelmed, and I've always found these charterers willing to both listen and share their advice in good spirits.

The second type of charterer is a member of the dreaded flotilla. A flotilla experience is where you travel with a convoy of other boats. A designated fleet captain does all the planning, deciding where you go and where you anchor. One condition of joining a flotilla is that you must obey the fleet captain. Typically, the members of flotillas are new and inexperienced skippers who value the help and guidance of their fleet captain. It's not a terrible idea on paper, but I dislike that flotillas remove personal responsibility from the individual skipper. Unfortunately, the fleet captains aren't always that experienced either; occasionally, they barely have more experience than the skippers in the boats they are guiding.

As we enjoyed our drinks, a small sailing boat pulled into the cove and anchored beside where we were all lined up stern-to. A minor concern — given the angle of their chain, they'd probably dropped their anchor over another boat's anchor, but it happens. We'd seen this boat previously in another harbour, and from the various charter flags flying from their topping lift, it was clear they were the fleet captain for a flotilla about to arrive.

Sure enough, they launched their tender and then moments later, a series of identical sailing boats started entering the bay. The tender started running around, directing all the boats on where to anchor. They instructed one of the boats to drop anchor and back down between *Matilda* and Kerry and Keven's boat.

A young family was aboard, and as they tied off, I chatted with the Dad at the helm, "You know, I'm not sure if this is a good spot for you. I don't think your chain is set properly, and the wind has been whipping up here in the afternoon across the bow to thirty knots."

He looked a little worried, then shrugged apologetically, "Sorry! I have to stay here; this is where the fleet captain told me to go."

It's this combination of inexperience while being beholden to another captain who's not on their boat that makes flotillas dangerous. We now had a boat anchored beside us that was a concern, and the skipper, while friendly enough, couldn't and wouldn't do anything about it without permission. I waved the fleet captain over, who came by in his tender.

"Mate, I don't think this is safe. This boat is going to lose its anchor when the wind picks up and crash into our boat."

The fleet captain just shrugged and sped off to help the next flotilla member. Conditions were currently good, and to be charitable to him, he'd probably dealt with entitled people protecting their position in anchorages all week. He still had another eight boats to get anchored up.

He immediately anchored another catamaran on the far side of Keven and Kerry in the shallow water. This time, there was no doubt the anchor chain was placed over theirs, with nowhere near enough length for the impending conditions.

We continued to watch the drama unfold. The windlass on one of the boats wouldn't work (a familiar story), so it was tied up alongside the fleet captain's boat. Yet another potential disaster waiting to happen, as they now had double the weight on the one anchor.

Before long, exactly as had happened the previous two evenings, the wind began to pick up, and the boat next to us started to slip sideways. Their anchor quickly came loose, and they began to push into *Matilda*. We already had our fenders out, which prevented any damage, but the weight of the wind and their boat pressing on us now meant we were likely to lose our anchor, too.

Keven looked at me and said, "It's good you had those fenders out already."

I turned to him, frustrated at the situation unfolding before us. "I'm a god-damned clairvoyant. I tell you, this is precisely what I predicted would happen!".

"Well, what do you think is going to happen next?" he asked.

"That catamaran on the other side of you is going to lose its anchor and decide to pull out. They will pull up your anchor as they go, and you'll be in trouble, too."

"Well shit, I better get back to the boat then!" Keven quickly grabbed Kerry, and they hustled off into their tender to return to their boat.

Ouch. Well, that was obvious. I felt like an idiot for not raising it sooner. I'd been sitting back watching the potential disaster unfold but hadn't been anywhere near proactive enough in acting on it.

By the time Kerry and Keven grabbed their gear and hopped back into their tender, the anchorage was quickly becoming a disaster zone. As predicted, the catamaran lost its hold, started hauling in their anchor, and promptly hauled up Keven and Kerry's.

Keven and Kerry only managed to save the rear of their boat from hitting the shore by jamming their tender in between it and the rocks as a makeshift fender. All I could do was watch as they desperately tried to board and start their engines while the catamaran floundered around just off their bow, pulling at their anchor chain with a stuck anchor.

While all this was happening, I finally decided we needed to act before things got any worse. I yelled to Karina, "Start the motors now. We're getting out of here."

The boat beside us was pushing us more as the wind gusted harder. Our anchor started to slip, and we were slowly being forced sideways towards the fancy superyacht on our port side.

With the motors on, we quickly stabilised, pulling forward against the ropes.

"OK, I need you to stay up on the helm. I'm going to jump in and free the stern lines," I said. "I'll bring in the leeward[1] side first, then as soon as the windward side is clear, you motor out away, pulling up the anchor from here."

There was a major problem with this plan that I didn't think about until it was too late.

I jumped in, swam to shore and freed the leeward line, bringing it back on board without difficulty. *Matilda* was now held by the windward line, and what little hold was still being provided by our anchor. Then, I jumped back into the water to free the windward line from the shore.

It mostly went to plan. With the lines removed, *Matilda* started to move forward out of the mess. Karina was manoeuvring carefully, avoiding the boats on both sides. The large boat on our starboard side was yelling something at her that we couldn't hear over the wind. The fleet captain was racing around in his tender, using it to push the boat on our fenders away from our port side.

It's about now I realised the problem with my plan. *Matilda* was pulling away, and I was still in the water. It's not the safest place to be, with boats moving around in chaos.

As I swam after *Matilda*, Karina was actively working to keep her from hitting boats that I couldn't see, and so I decided that moving forward until she was well clear was the best call. All I knew was that as fast as I could swim, *Matilda* kept getting further away.

Eventually, Karina had *Matilda* far enough forward that although the anchor wasn't yet retrieved, *Matilda* was clear of nearby boats around her and safely under Karina's control at the helm. Free of our support, the yacht that caused the issues was now rapidly moving sideways towards the large motor yacht while trying to clear their lines and leave as well.

I'd been shouting out to Karina as she navigated forward, and now, with the boat safe, she turned back to look at me and called out, "What is it you want me to do?"

"Stop the boat so I can get back on board!"

The anchorage erupted in laughter. Despite the chaos among our small corner of four or five boats, another ten boats were still secured safely to shore, their crews up on the bow watching things unfold. We'd just become the next blockbuster episode of Harbour Cinema. Finally, safely back on board, I retrieved the remaining floating stern line, and we headed for the open sea.

---

1. The side away from the wind. You typically release the lines on this side first as the windward side takes the pressure.

When you've been through an emergency, the adrenaline rush, followed by the crash, can be overwhelming. Our hearts were racing, and we both felt sick. Outside the bay and safely cruising forward on autopilot, I called a break.

"Let's take five," I said.

Far better to calm down. The immediate emergency was over, and trying to make decisions in this agitated state wouldn't go well.

We cruised for five minutes or so, dried off, grabbed a water and then, once we'd calmed down, decided what to do.

Kerry and Keven had messaged us; they were safe. They'd snagged their prop with a stern line, but they managed to drop their anchor again and get tied off. We learnt later that the flotilla, which came in and wreaked havoc, finally decided the conditions were no good, so they all pulled out and headed to a nearby port instead.

It was still light, although the sun was starting to set. There was another anchorage just a couple of miles around the corner, so we decided to head there, but we also made a Plan B just in case that wasn't a viable option.

Plan A: Head to the new anchorage and find a spot there.

Plan B: Keep heading north for another hour to an anchorage outside a port town that was certain to be calm.

Thankfully, Plan A worked. The next anchorage was much calmer than where we'd left. We dropped the anchor and started to back down. When we were set, I took the floating stern line and started to pay it out over the edge, ready for me to hop in the water and swim it to shore.

I glanced over to check the progress, fully expecting the bright yellow line to be floating on the surface like normal, only to see the end of it sinking beneath the water back under the boat.

"Go to neutral!" I screamed to the helm, where Karina was piloting.

Too late. There was a crunch, and the port engine juddered to a halt, stalling the motor as the rope wrapped the propellor and jammed the shaft. I'd left the heavy snatch strap, which protects the lines from the rocks, still attached to the end. In my tired and stressed state, I never considered that it was heavy enough to drag the line back under the water instead of floating on the surface.

"Fuuuuuck!!!"

I don't think I've ever felt as despondent about the choices we'd made than at that moment. We were stuck with one engine out of commission. Fortunately, the anchor was set, but our small bay had no swing room. We had to either continue tying off to the shore or pull up the anchor and leave on one engine. With darkness approaching and no idea about the state of the propellor, which still had rope wrapped around it, it seemed the best bet was to continue with the plan to stay overnight.

I cut and cleared away the line I could easily access, which left me just enough length to reach the shore with the remainder. After another fifteen minutes, we were finally secured, safe enough for now.

With darkness finally descending and the boat secured, I tried diving on the propellor to clear the rest of the line. I couldn't free the rest of the rope from around the propellor, so we called it a night. We had a lovely meal, enjoyed the stars and went to bed.

The plan for the morning was to try and free the propellor ourselves once we were well-rested and in daylight. If that failed, we would limp on one engine to a nearby port and find a diver to remove it for us.

Fortunately, we didn't need to. A superyacht arrived overnight and wanted to take our spot. We explained to the captain that we were having issues, so they sent one of their crew over to dive and free the propellor for us! Thirty minutes later, the propellor was released. We ran some basic tests, and then we were back underway.

I won't lie; I wanted to blame the flotilla for our problems, but what we took away from this experience is three critical lessons:

1. If you know something's wrong, act, and act early! We saw the issues with the flotilla as it came in and even predicted precisely what would happen. The fact that we remained in place until it did was our fault. We should have pulled anchor and left before it all went to hell.

2. Process and procedure! We had a good process for setting the stern lines that worked well, but when we had to escape quickly, we hadn't reset them correctly. We'd never have hooked the propellor if I'd removed the snatch straps. Now, we have a process we follow every time we bring them back on board — no thinking, just doing it consistently.

3. Be prepared to let things go. We set our ropes with snatch straps and tie them back to the boat EXACTLY for this emergency. The ropes can be pulled back aboard from *Matilda*, while the snatch straps (approx. €10 each) remain on shore to be abandoned or retrieved later. If I'd stuck to this plan and sacrificed the snatch straps, it would have been safer without me entering the water, and

we wouldn't have snagged the propellor.

Confidence leads to over-confidence, but if you can survive the missteps, you'll be a better sailor and better prepared. We've tripped over ourselves more times than I care to recount here, but we've also tried to learn the lessons.

As Elias, the harbour master in Porto Cheli, would say, "You got better; that's what matters. Not everyone gets better!"

***

With all the drama, where is the joy? The reality is that no one wants to read a story of the sea where the bulk of the action is punctuated with "and then nothing happened."

Fortunately, you'll never hear such a bland tale of sunny days when talking to a liveaboard cruiser. There's nothing a sailor loves more than sharing exaggerated stories. Our interactions with each other are interspersed with "You won't believe what happened when...", "We saw that too..." or "You think that's bad..."

Yet, if endless drama and adventure were all it was, most of us would never do it. The fact is that most of the time, nothing happens. Weather forecasts are consulted, charts reviewed, pilot guides and online reviews of anchorages analysed in depth. We set off in the weather windows well within the capabilities of our boats and ourselves and safely make it from one port to another. Our worst days are quickly put behind us, then celebrated as tales to tell over a beer in port the next day, moving from sheer, gut-wrenching terror to something worthy of a good laugh over drinks.

The reality is we live this lifestyle because we love it! It has its challenges, and there is always a small risk of injury[2], but life or boat-threatening incidents are incredibly rare.

***

So what does nothing happening look like? What keeps us coming back? One of the simplest pleasures is a comfortable journey from anchorage to anchorage. It varies from

---

2. Only yesterday, I came down the stairs in a hurry and kicked myself in the back of the calf, cutting myself with my toenail!

boat to boat what that looks like, but even those of us on powerboats can generally agree with sailboats that a nice warm day, calm seas and a cool breeze is ideal[3].

When you arrive in a sheltered anchorage with light winds and no swell, most sailors will tell you they sleep better on a boat than onshore. After a day spent outdoors, swimming, sailing and chatting until the sun goes down, we're happy to collapse into bed. There's a familiarity with the sounds of a boat, and by and large, you sleep deeply and soundly with the gentle rocking motion of a boat at rest.

One of my favourite times is the early morning, sitting up at the flybridge with a fresh ground coffee and watching the sunrise. A gentle nod and a shared moment with the other early risers on their boats, sitting out on their swim deck, enjoying the same feeling of peace while others sleep below. There's no need for a shower to prepare for the day; just step off the swim deck and enjoy the crystal clear, calm waters with a stunning island as a backdrop. Then, a quick wash down with the freshwater shower, and you're done, ready to go and cruise for the day.

While we don't always see large sea life, it's exciting when we do. It could be a school of flying fish when the water is calm, flitting out of the sea and dancing along the surface before diving back below. In some parts of Greece, sea turtles are a frequent hazard, often spotted in the distance basking in the sun, one flipper in the air – is it a buoy, a log? No, it's a turtle. By the time you recognise it, they flip and dive beneath the surface.

The highlight is, of course, dolphins, a frequent visitor in certain areas. It might just be a fin or two in the distance as they make their way through the sea, but with luck, they'll come by to visit. We used to slow the boat when that happened, but our best experiences are when we are going at a steady pace — the dolphins are happy and more than capable of keeping up and dancing through the bow wave. They seem to enjoy the challenge.

A Greek charter skipper once said, "The dolphins stay longer if you are calm and peaceful."

I cocked an eyebrow sceptically. "Are you sure? To be honest, I haven't noticed a difference."

"You try cruising with a group of eight young ladies — trust me, the dolphins are more enjoyable when everyone is quiet".

---

3. Although we are okay with a little less wind than the sailboats.

We now tell our guests the same. The experience is enhanced by quietly standing at the bow and watching them play in the waves beneath it without the squeals of "OMG DOLPHINS!!!!"

Superyachts ply the waters, too. Rampant excess, but always exciting to see. We spot them on AIS, look them up online and find pictures of what they might look like inside and, of course, what they cost to charter.

"€800,000 a week for 12 guests! Who has that kind of money?" From my previous life in Silicon Valley, even the tiny handful of people I know who could afford it without concern are too sensible to blow that kind of money on a week's holiday.

We chug away at 6.5 knots, cruising to our destination and enjoying the sun and the sights. We'll swap roles every hour or two, allowing the other of us to snooze in the sun, get something to eat or relax. Eventually, we arrive — most of the time, within only a few hours of leaving.

If everything has gone to plan, we'll be at the anchorage early enough that we can have the pick of where we want to be. One of us, usually Karina, will head up to the bow to spot the perfect place. On a good day and in the right location, the waters are typically clear enough to see the bottom easily, even when it's 10 metres deep.

Then, it's time to drop the anchor, making sure it's set correctly. Backing down, on this perfect day, the anchor will bite the first time, and the chain stretch taut, the boat straining against the anchor now buried deeply into the sand.

This is the simple joy of cruising. Despite the many tales of woe and disasters that seemed to unfold along the way, the reality is that most of our time heading north through the Ionian felt something like this.

We made friends in many places, exchanging "boat cards" (business cards for your boat) with critical information like boat name, our names, contact numbers and a photo of you and your boat as a reminder.

After two seasons cruising, my phone is full of contacts, from complete details of people and boats to a simple name, "Adam", that I can't recollect. Occasionally, I now receive WhatsApp messages at Christmas with a canned electronic card sent to all contacts wishing a Merry Christmas (or from our US friends, Happy Holidays) and a Happy New Year. It can take a moment to remember who they were and where we met them, but it's fun to be reminded even fleetingly of the adventures during summer.

Given all the choices, a warm Summer's day on a boat, reading, swimming and napping while listening to the goats is one of the best ways to spend your time.

***

Even when things don't go as planned, don't underestimate the satisfaction and joy that comes from problem-solving and achieving something against the odds.

I don't love being seasick, and maybe I wouldn't make the same choices again, but I've generally never truly regretted the decisions that have led us into rougher seas. The sense of accomplishment in having tackled and conquered what nature had to throw our way leaves us with a sense of pride. We've pushed the envelope on our skills and experiences, making us better prepared for next time. And, when you've been through a challenging experience, that feeling of arriving into a harbour you know and trust is incredible. There's a deep feeling of satisfaction in knowing the boat and crew are safe. We succeeded in what we set out to do.

Each season leaves us both feeling more and more confident about what we can achieve. We now mostly enjoy a challenge.

Aside from the weather, boats are full of systems that, as we've well established, are determined to break for the most minor reasons. Coming from an industry where change can take months to years to make happen, there's immense satisfaction in diagnosing an issue and fixing it efficiently. From shaky beginnings as a novice, *Matilda* and I know each other well now. Each new thing that fails is an excuse to learn more, get my hands dirty, and build confidence that I can resolve the simple problems we might encounter daily.

***

There's also joy in very unexpected things too!

One of ours is our washing machine. While a washing machine is becoming common on modern cruising boats, plenty of older boats (and charter boats) are without them. As cruisers, access to an easy way to wash clothes is a sought-after commodity.

You can bet that it will be one of the featured items on any tour of a boat with a washing machine. The cupboard where it's stored opened with a flourish to show the precious device. We are no exception.

Whenever we meet new friends, one of our first offers is, "If you want to do some washing, just let us know."

While it's an odd offer, given that we have a generator and a water maker on board, it's not a drama for us. We're typically not that short on the critical resources of water and power.

People rarely say yes on the first offer, but we've made plenty of cruiser friends who, once they know us a bit better, sheepishly come around the next day to ask, "So, about that washing machine..."

Once, we pulled into a harbour, and a sailboat shouted, "We have some laundry for you!"

At the time, I thought it was kind of rude, and I was trying to work out if it was an insult towards a motorboat. Then Karina remembered who they were. We'd met them the week before and offered the loan of our washing machine. Into the second week of their charter with two young kids on board, the washing machine became a more valuable commodity than they'd planned for!

Karina also enjoys cooking, although it's fair to say that she doesn't love the gas oven on *Matilda*, which can be temperamental at best. Still, after a couple of seasons, she's figured out most of the quirks to the point that she can make it do many of the things she'd like. It will never bake a soufflé, but it will turn out a mean chocolate chip cookie.

This is how one wet and rainy afternoon late in the season, we came to have two large plates of fresh-from-the-oven cookies, and only two of us to eat them. Looking around the anchorage, Karina spotted a tender coming back to the only other boat with people on board.

"Go call them over," she said. It's long-established in our relationship that while Karina is happy to be social, I'm the social coordinator. All the contacts of the people and boats we meet are on my phone, and if there are new people to meet, it's on me to break the ice.

I popped out onto the swim deck and waved to catch their attention. The Dad dropped everyone back on their boat and came by on the tender.

"What's the matter?" he asked hesitantly. He was concerned perhaps that we had some issue with their boat placement in the anchorage.

"We just had some extra cookies," I said, passing him a paper plate full of cookies with our boat card balanced on top.

"Uh. Thanks."

We chatted briefly; then he gingerly drove the tender back to his boat, balancing the cookies, where his very excited 6-year-old son took the plate, waved wildly at us and then disappeared inside the boat. They left early the next day, and that was it.

It was the following season, almost 600 nautical miles away from that anchorage, a man on a tender I didn't recognise pulled up behind our swim deck.

"Hey Tim, how are you and Karina?"

I'm getting good at faking conversations with people I don't recognise by now. "We're great, how are you?"

"Yeah, we're doing well. Just wanted to say thanks again for the cookies; they were fantastic."

While liveaboard life has its challenges, there's nothing — absolutely nothing — half so much worth doing as simply messing about in boats. And it's the people that you meet and the experiences you share that make for moments of pure joy.

Sixteen

The beginning

"Every new beginning comes from some other beginning's end."—
Seneca

From starting as keyboard-bound desk jockeys to increasingly competent sailors, we were living our dream. We had navigated our way from the cutting edge of technology and the future in Silicon Valley to slow down and become part of a community and way of life as old as the first person who set to sea. No longer techies, we had become full-time boat bums.

As the end of our second season approached, we were ready for yet more challenges. Having made our way to the island of Corfu, at the north end of the Ionian Sea, and of Greece, we weren't ready to stop. It was tantalising to realise that if we continued, we could explore Croatia and Italy. Famous cities like Dubrovnik, Split, Trieste, and Venice were all within reach if we could keep pushing forward and head north.

***

The dreamers talk of casting free to explore the world, while the doers are out there already, cruising and enjoying life and tackling challenges as they arise. They are learning and improving, taking risks, getting better and discovering more about what they do and don't like.

You may not be ready or able to step into a 50-foot monohull that's only a few years old, fully equipped and ready to sail the world. But you can find a boat out there, which will let you start doing — whatever that looks like. Maybe it's just exploring your local waters, taking a few overnights away and enjoying the company of friends.

Buying a boat is a manageable financial risk. With the ever-increasing numbers of people who want to make a change like this, the demand for new boats is so high that manufacturing timelines are pushing out to several years. Don't get me wrong, you'll spend plenty of money while you own a boat, although research and choosing the right one will help reduce that. After a year or two, if you decide this isn't the boat for you or that you've had your fill, there's a good chance you'll recoup close to the initial purchase price and, lately, perhaps a little more.

Perhaps, instead of cruising the world, it's tackling a well-travelled cruising ground, buying an older, smaller boat from a couple that's had their fill. Now, you've got a base to explore Greece and the Eastern Mediterranean for a few years while you decide if this is the lifestyle for you. Whatever it is, there's a way to get started that will work with your resources and risk levels.

As we reflect, Karina and I know that despite the challenges, the hesitations, and the lessons experienced along the way, there's nothing we'd rather be doing today than exploring the coast by boat.

We rushed into it too fast. I'd had some experience, but probably not enough. Despite having the basic knowledge of sailing and navigating a boat, I knew absolutely nothing about the intricacies and challenges of owning one. Which I still think overall is a good thing — some things really can only be learnt by doing. We stopped dreaming, started doing it, and we made it happen.

If a couple of office workers can throw it all in to go live on the sea, then a thousand different professions have you better prepared for the realities than us.

We don't know where it goes from here, but we know that our foreseeable plans involve a boat to one degree or another. Whether moving on to the canals in France with a canal barge, selling *Matilda* here in the Mediterranean to buy a monohull in the Caribbean or switching hemispheres to explore Australia and Asia. We're confident that for the next several years, at least, we'll be on a boat.

Which is a good thing.

Despite the challenges thrown at us along the way, the money we've wasted on things we later realised we didn't need, and a constant obsession with the weather, we're convinced. Of all the things we could be doing, there's nothing quite so liberating as being aboard a boat.

Our journey's just beginning.

— THE END —

Meet the author

 **Tim Bull** lives with his wife Karina on their boat, *Matilda*, in the Mediterranean. Together, they are constantly learning new and exciting ways to break things. He has two grown children who are far more sensible than him. He enjoys travelling, playing with gadgets and writing. Tim writes weekly about his adventures travelling and exploring the world at timbull.com. You can sign up for regular updates there. Matilda has her own Instagram account, @matildatheboat. If you enjoyed the book, please leave a review. It's the best way to support the author and help others discover it.

Acknowledgements

No author writes alone, and I've been amazed at just how much of a team effort even a self-published book can be!

First and foremost, there would be no book without Viv. Thank you for the encouragement to turn my weekly musings about living aboard into a book. He read every draft, from the first few chapters right up to the last final edit. Every project needs a biggest fan.

Judy of Sailing *Fair Isle*, thank you for your detailed critique and great suggestions. You made it a better book.

Chris, who has her own series of travel books, provided some great advice about the importance of characters. Thank you for the guidance.

Many people read drafts and provided feedback, thank you all. But, I do want to call out Linda and Sarah. Your cheerleading kept me going when it became challenging.

My daughter, Ella, was the brutal critic that I needed. Her frank, honest and constructive feedback was the catalyst I needed to make some important changes.

My son Jasper, as always, made me laugh, and his feedback that the book was "unexpectedly good" gave me hope.

Finally, Karina. There is no book without you. Beyond being the reason there is an adventure to write about in the first place, your attention to detail and willingness to spend days hunting down every small inconsistency in the text was invaluable.

Thank you to everyone who was been a part of our adventures so far.

Amazing Creators

Please take a moment to support these amazing creators.

Judy and Steve of Sailing *Fair Isle* - Judy and Steve create incredible YouTube videos every week about their life sailing on *Fair Isle*. Thank you Judy for your kind review and words for the book. You'll find them on YouTube – search for @svfairisle.

Henk-Jan of MV Lady Liselot - If the author could create YouTube content about his life on *Matilda*, he would be thrilled if it was half as entertaining as Henk-Jan's tales of life on his trawler *MV Lady Liselot*. Find him on YouTube – search for @MVLadyLiselot.

Iain and Kate of Intrepid Bear - You're always welcome aboard Matilda. In the meantime, they share their life aboard *Intrepid Bear* on YouTube – search for @FollowIntrepidBear.

Jasna - When she's not solo sailing through the Adriatic, she can be found online at jasnatuta.com where she has several very popular books of her own.

Philipp is well on the way to his dream aluminium ketch. Check out what he's up to on Instagram @philipp_sailing.

Chris writes books and creates videos about travel and launching into nomadic life. You can find her and her husband Steve online at EatWalkLearn.com.

Printed in Great Britain
by Amazon

36756174R00101